ACTION REAR

Voices of the 2nd Battalion, The Royal Warwickshire Regiment: D-Day and Normandy Campaign 1944

Christopher Cox

Helion & Company Limited

Helion & Company Limited
Unit 8 Amherst Business Centre
Budbrooke Road
Warwick
CV34 5WE
England
Tel. 01926 499619
Email: info@helion.co.uk
Website: www.helion.co.uk
X (formerly Twitter): @Helionbooks
Facebook: @HelionBooks
Visit our blog at helionbooks.wordpress.com

Published by Helion & Company 2025
Designed and typeset by Mach 3 Solutions (www.mach3solutions.co.uk)
Cover designed by Paul Hewitt, Battlefield Design (www.battlefield-design.co.uk)

ISBN 978-1-804518-13-7

British Library Cataloguing-in-Publication Data.
A catalogue record for this book is available from the British Library.

For Charlie,

We will always re[illegible] you when
th[illegible]orgets

Field Marshal Bernard Law Montgomery, 1st Viscount Montgomery of Alamein, KG, GCB, DSO, PC, DL

I know the Warwickshire soldier well.
I know his virtues and I know his faults, and when you weigh them up what a wide margin of virtue is found.
There is no better soldier

Contents

Acknowledgements

It is with the greatest of appreciation that I tender my thanks to the following individuals and organisations for supporting this project.

Duncan Rogers and Helion & Company, for supporting my project and the partnership in publishing this work.
Sarah, Hazel and Edie, for encouraging me and putting up with 'Daddy's War Waffle'.
Ernie Tweed, for his family insights and providing such a trove of photographs.
Nick Smalley, for providing a copy of the letter written by Charlie Tweed to his sister Jessie.
Claire Linsell, for her time and support with my research and for introducing me to her grandfather, Captain Peter Batt.
Rob Pettitt, for his advice, the invaluable video interview with his father, Private Sir Dennis Pettitt, and for access to an incredible file of letters, photographs and newspaper clippings his father kept.
Lindsay Brooks & Deb Richardson, for providing a fantastic source of references kept by their grandfather, Private John Gundy, and for creating the 'Finding Buck' documentary.
Abi Rutland-Turner, for her support and for her insights into her grandfather, Private Walter Charles Gray, and the records created by the family. And for amazing me with her family's history in the Second World War.
The Illing family, for their support and kind permission to source the excellent *No Better Soldier* by Harry Illing.
Lieutenant Colonel John Rice and Major Charles Illing for their support and for providing Harry Illing's battlefield tour notes, audio recordings and the 'Tiny' Adams account.
Jason Woods and The Royal Warwickshire Regiment Re-enactment Group for providing so many photographs of members of the battalion and for the incredible work they do to remember the battalion.
The Bannerman family, for their support and kind permission to access the wonderful *If I Don't Come Home – Letters from D-Day* by Alastair Bannerman.
Will Thatcher for sharing his incredible knowledge with me and providing the audio account of Sergeant Bob Barnett.
Markus Reisner and Andreas Hartinger for their kind permission to use extracts from *D-Day Tank Hunter* by Hans Hoeller.

The Lee family for the fantastic work they had done in researching their father/grandfather Captain J. Lee, and for allowing me to access that work.

Andrew Williams for his kind permission to use extracts from his excellent *D-Day to Berlin*.

Anette Fuhrmeister and The History Press for their kind permission to use extracts from John Lincoln's *Thank God and The Infantry*.

Harriett Feilding, Pen & Sword Books and Frontline Books for their kind permission to use extracts from *Panzer Commander* by Hans von Luck.

Stephen Fisher for his kind permission to use extracts from his excellent *Sword Beach*.

Amy Durant and Sapere Books for their kind permission to use extracts from *Caen: Anvil of Victory* by Alexander KcKee.

The Royal Regiment of Fusiliers Museum Warwick, for an inexhaustible amount of information. To Chris Kirby for allowing me the opportunity to volunteer at the museum, and especially to David Baynham, for his guidance and for being a bottomless source of military history facts and detail.

The Royal Regiment of Fusiliers, Tidworth Barracks, for allowing me access and to photograph the Soloman painting.

The National Archives, Kew, for the work they do to record Second World War diaries.

Imperial War Museum for being such an incredible source of audio, video and photographic resources and for the licensing agreement for the sources referenced in this work. All copyright and other rights in the Imperial War Museum files referenced in this work are, and remain, the property of the IWM.

Commonwealth War Graves Commission for making the details of fallen soldiers so accessible to their families and the nation.

The museums for the East Surrey Regiment, Royal Army Chaplains and Military Medicine for their support.

Facebooks groups for Royal Warwickshire Regiment World War 2, D-Day Marshalling and Embarkation areas research group, 3rd Infantry Division "Iron sides" for the support of their members.

A final thank you to all veterans of the Royal Warwickshire Regiment for their service to the United Kingdom and anybody who has supported the Royal Regiment of Fusiliers Museum Warwick.

Comparative Military Ranks

British Army	Heer	Waffen-SS
Private	Schütze/Grenadier/Oberschütze	SS-Schütze/ SS-Oberschütze
Lance Corporal	Gefreiter	SS-Sturmmann
Corporal	Obergefreiter	SS-Rottenführer
Lance Sergeant	Unteroffizier	SS-Unterscharführer
Sergeant	Unterfeldwebel	SS-Scharführer
Colour/staff Sergeant	Feldwebel	SS-Oberscharführer
Sergeant Major – WO2	Oberfeldwebel	SS-Hauptscharführer
Sergeant Major – WO1	Hauptfeldwebel	SS-Sturmscharführer
Second Lieutenant	Leutnant	SS-Untersturmführer
Lieutenant	Oberleutnant	SS-Obersturmführer
Captain	Hauptmann	SS-Hauptsturmführer
Major	Major	SS-Sturmbannführer
Lieutenant Colonel	Oberstleutnant	SS-Obersturmbannführer
Colonel	Oberst	SS-Standartenführer
Brigadier	Generalmajor	SS-Brigadeführer
Major-General	Generalleutnant	SS-Gruppenführer
Lieutenant-General	General	SS-Obergruppenführe
General	Generaloberst	SS-Oberstgruppenführer
Field Marshal	Generalfeldmarschall	(none)

Abbreviations

2iC	Second in Command
AA	Anti-aircraft
AT	Anti-tank
AVRE	Assault Vehicles Royal Engineers
BEF	British Expeditionary Force (to France in 1939)
BLA	British Liberation Army
CMP	Corps of Military Police
CO	Commanding Officer
Coy	Company
CSM	Company Sergeant-Major
CWGC	Commonwealth War Graves Commission
DSO	Distinguished Service Order
ENSA	Entertainments National Service Association
FDS	Field Dressing Station
GOC	General Officer Commanding
HQ	Headquarters
IO	Intelligence Officer
KIA	Killed in Action
KOSB	King's Own Scottish Borderers
KSLI	King's Shropshire Light Infantry
LCI	Landing Craft Infantry (L for large, S for small)
LCT	Landing Craft Tank
L of C	Lines of Communication
MC	Military Cross
MG	Machine gun
MIA	Missing in Action
MM	Military Medal
MO	Medical Officer
NAAFI	Navy, Army, Air Force Institute
NCO	Non-commissioned Officer

OBE	Order of the British Empire
O Group	Orders Group
OC	Officer Commanding
OK West	Oberkommando West – Supreme Command West
OKW	Oberkommando der Wehrmacht
QM	Quartermaster
RA	Royal Artillery
RACD	Royal Army Chaplains' Department
RAMC	Royal Army Medical Corps
RASC	Royal Army Service Corps
RCAF	Royal Canadian Air Force
RE	Royal Engineers
SO	Signals Officer
SP	Self-propelled
WO	Warrant Officer
WREN	Women's Royal Naval Service
X Craft	British midget submarines

Preface

Thank you for taking the time and expense to read this book. My hope in writing this work is to bring back to life some of the men of the Royal Warwickshire Regiment who fought and died in the service of their King and Country, to hear again their voices and for those relatives left behind to have something tangible to hold representing those men's achievements and bravery. The aim of the book is not to celebrate victory over another nation, but to show pride in the sacrifices our forebears made for us.

I am proud to have two generations of Royal Warwickshire Regiment veterans from two World Wars in my family and take great pleasure in supporting, as a volunteer, the regimental museum, now the Royal Regiment of Fusiliers Museum Warwick. All proceeds from the sale of this work will be donated to the Museum.

This work isn't a history of D-Day, it is an account of the 2nd Battalion Royal Warwickshire Regiment, specifically in the memory of a single man's experience of the invasion of Normandy.

Corporal Charles Tweed was my Great Uncle, my maternal grandfathers' brother. Nor is this a first-hand account, for Great Uncle Charlie, as with countless thousands of other brothers, husbands, fathers and uncles, did not return from Normandy, he now lies in Douvres Le Délivrande Commonwealth War Graves Cemetery. My grandfather never spoke of him; indeed, I did not even know of him until after my grandfather had passed away.

I regret not having the gumption to start this project as a younger man, when there were still veterans alive and my family members to speak to in person, and understand their lives first-hand. My grandparents did not talk about the war, the only recollection I have is of my grandmother, Betty, upon seeing a full moon one evening in the car, calling it a 'bomber's moon' and explaining that during the war she was able to differentiate a German bomber from a British aeroplane by the different sounds of their engines as they flew overhead at night. As I write, there is just one member of the Royal Warwickshire Regiment who served during the Second World War alive, Norman Smith nears his 100th birthday, but sadly he is unable to contribute to this narrative.

Despite detailed research, I do not suggest I am pre-eminent on this subject, I am only as knowledgeable as the sources I have thus far found, and I am sure there is far more for me to learn. I actively encourage readers to please contact me via e-mail (see below) with any questions, corrections or additional information and sources to grow the wider understanding of this subject. My greatest hope is to discover an account out there that references my Great Uncle Charlie.

Christopher Cox
actionrearbook1944@yahoo.com

1

Prologue

Charlie is cold, uncomfortable and sick. It is Monday 5 June 1944, already sat on board the troop ship since the previous day, the weather and the rough sea at Newhaven combined with the pervasive smell of vomit are taking their toll and adding to the anxiety of not knowing if or where they are about to go. 23-year-old Lance Corporal Charles Tweed, along with the rest of the 2nd Battalion Royal Warwickshire Regiment are already on their landing ships, desperately waiting for 'it' to start. The invasion of North-West Europe has been delayed, they should already be there, and the waiting is fraying their nerves. June 1944 saw some of the worst weather in the Channel for 20 years, even for an English summer it was bad. The cold, rain and wind had been persistent for days now and it was difficult to see how it was going to improve. But it was about to, if only slightly.

At the outbreak of war Charlie was a 17-year-old stone-quarry man. Born on 31 August 1921 and brought up in Atherstone, North Warwickshire, in a working class mining community, Charlie was the sixth of eleven largely neglected children. Life had been hard for, and because of, his parents, William and Jessie. Early life for the Tweed children was interspersed with periods of true hardship and peppered with court dates for their parents. In 1923, William and Jessie were summoned to court for child neglect. The NSPCC had inspected the family home in Lagoe's Buildings in Atherstone and found it to be 'not fit for pigs to live in yet alone children' and the children '…dirty, flesh and clothing, their heads verminous and bodies flea bitten.'[1] Even for a period where slums and cramped living conditions were not uncommon, this was sobering to read of my own family. In 1927 and 1935 my Great-Grandparents were again taken to court, this time for failing to send their children, including my grandfather Arthur, to school regularly. As a possible slight mitigation, William Tweed had witnessed the horrors of the trenches in the Great War, which I am convinced must have scarred all veterans in one way or another and may have influenced his behaviour. Like his sons, he had served with the Royal Warwickshire Regiment, the 10th Battalion in his case, he received 'gunshot wounds' while serving in France and once recovered was transferred to the Royal Engineers. Bill, Charlie's brother, older by two years, was a pre-war regular

1 *The Nuneaton Chronicle & Midland Farmers Gazette*, 2 November 1923, p.8.

with the Royal Engineers, seeing action in North Africa, Italy and North-West Europe during the Second World War.

Charlie had missed the so-called 'Phoney War,' the shock of the retreat through France and the horror of the Dunkirk beaches. He had originally enlisted on 6 November 1940 and had been posted to the Royal East Surrey Regiment before being transferred to the Royal Warwickshire Regiment on 11 March 1942. Exact details of his war service are limited, sadly his service records cannot be found either in the Ministry of Defence Archives or in The National Archives at Kew. Even service number 6143733 on Charlie's headstone appears to be incorrect. His service number at the point of transfer to the Warwick's was 6148733, this number is shown on the Graves Concentration Report from December 1944, but the eight has been crossed out and a handwritten three inserted above it.

I have, where possible, used direct first-hand accounts to provide a closer narrative from the men who were there (their word is worth far more than mine ever could be) and provided the context around them from the research of the last few years.

Most of the servicemen referenced served with the Royal Warwickshire Regiment, although I have also used sources from the accompanying forces around them, particularly the 1st Battalion Royal Norfolk Regiment, who served alongside them, especially for periods where sources from the Warwickshires are limited. Some of the accounts sourced within this work were written down or recorded many years after the events, so with time and as our memory changes, especially after such traumatic events, we must be understanding if any of the times, dates or places do not necessarily match perfectly with either others accounts or the official documentation already in existence.

As Charlie sat there, one can only imagine what he was thinking about. Young men dream of glory, was there a sense of adventure and excitement? Was there fear? Or I suspect more likely, was he thinking about Joan? His wife back in Atherstone, to whom he had been married for only 2 years, perhaps contemplating their future together, would there be a future? For the vast majority of the division this was their first time in action after many years of training on home soil, was there just the nagging question of 'are we up to the task in hand?' How would they react to coming under fire for the first time? Could they kill and ultimately, would they live?

2

Background

The 2nd Battalion Royal Warwickshire Regiment (2nd Warwicks), then part of 144th Infantry Brigade in 48th Infantry Division, had been posted to France in 1939, and after taking position in Belgium had suffered the ignominy of the retreat of 1940. This tragedy was epitomised by the heroic holding action at Wormhoudt, around 20km from Dunkirk, which enabled the bulk of the division to continue its escape towards the coast. The Warwicks, alongside sections of the Worcester Yeomanry, Cheshire Regiment and Royal Artillery held the elite *Waffen-SS Division Nr 1, Leibstandarte Adolf Hitler* for 24 hours, but with casualties rising and ammunition running short the defenders were forced to surrender on 28 May 1940. Despite expecting the decency of the Geneva Convention, the prisoners were rounded up in groups to be murdered, some having to dig their own grave before being shot. Around 90 were herded into a barn near Esquelbecq. Initially some were removed in groups of five and summarily shot; when this proved too onerous for the SS soldiers, grenades were hurled into barn in an attempt to murder all those inside, the barn was then sprayed with machine-gun fire. Over 200 men were killed that day at Wormhoudt, Ledringham and Esquelbecq, of which at least 70–90 were Warwicks,[1] a small number of men survived, were recaptured and were eventually able to return home, ensuring that the shocking details of the Wormhoudt Massacre were known.

The 2nd Battalion was not the only part of the regiment in action at this time. The 1st Battalion of the Royal Warwickshire Regiment was deployed to India and the Far East, to face enormously different, if no less challenging, circumstances. The 1/7th, 8th and 12th Battalions had also served in France and now embarked upon their own rebuilding and training journey in the UK. The 2nd Battalion was initially stationed in Devon on coastal defences duties, which, in the absence of an actual German invasion, held a lighter atmosphere for the men. Captain Illing had been posted to the 2nd Warwicks in 1940 as Carrier Platoon Commander and was now Officer Commanding A Company.

1 Guy Rommelaere (Shirley Wallis, trans.), *The Forgotten Massacre* (Warwick: Warwick Printing, 2001).

Captain Harry Illing
Officer Commanding A Company, 2nd Battalion Royal Warwickshire Regiment

> We had some wild men. Our Padre liked his tipple and was "pinched" for drinking after hours in the local pub. A subaltern – a newly appointed barrister – offered to defend him and did so on the singularly unfortunate basis of the Padre being an intimate friend and personal guest of the barmaid. No joy – a fine, headlines in the local newspaper and a rocket from the Bishop. At Christmas the Padre failed to turn up for church, it was not his fault, he had been rolled up in a carpet by our wildest subaltern and left immobilised in the mess ante-room. Regrettably neither stayed with us for long.
>
> Our first real excitement occurred during the invasion scare of 1940. Most of us were in a pub in Plymouth when the code word 'Cromwell' came through. Out we tumbled. We reached our war location in an orchard after a most difficult move, largely because the Home Guard with great enthusiasm had blocked everything. Inconsequentially we had kippers for breakfast, expecting to repel the German invader at any moment.

Come December 1940, 2nd Warwicks, now commanded by Major (Acting Lieutenant Colonel) Philip Hugh Whitby Hicks,[2] were transferred to Surrey as part of 24th Guards Independent Brigade Group. The battalion remained in Surrey until September 1942, whereupon they joined 185th Infantry Brigade in Ripon, before shortly, and finally, forming part of the British 3rd Infantry Division. Initially, the division expected to be part of the invasion of Sicily, but when this changed, Major General William Havelock Chaplin Ramsden, the then Divisional CO, secured the understanding that 3rd Division would spearhead the British invasion of North-West Europe when it came. As such the division was transferred to Scotland later in 1943, undergoing rigorous training for their eventual role in the return to the shores of France. Live fire beach assault and street fighting training was undertaken in Inverary, Kilbride, Aberdeen and Dorlin, and alongside other battalions they continually honed their skills with mock attacks on positions designed to replicate the strongpoints they would later face; while the realistic training made for excellent experience, it did not always run smoothly.

Brigadier Kenneth Pearce Smith
Officer Commanding 185th Infantry Brigade

> …each battalion had its own training programme. Each one of them had to undergo a fortnight's training at the Divisional Battle School at Moffat, ending up with a realistic attack, closely following an artillery barrage firing live shells, getting through wire and exploding phosphorous mines.
>
> Seeing a wretched soldier of the Warwicks, whose clothes were burning, I dashed to him and smothered the smouldering clothes with my hands, during

2 Later in the war as a Brigadier, Pip Hicks CBE, DSO & Bar, MC, born in Warwick, went on to lead First Air Landing Brigade, as part of the Allied invasion of Sicily and held a pivotal command during the battle for Arnhem.

which my right hand was slightly burnt. The soldier was hurried off to hospital. On my way back, I called in to see him and his burns were not serious and my hand was cleaned and bandaged.

Captain Harry Illing
Officer Commanding A Company, 2nd Battalion Royal Warwickshire Regiment

We got into our Landing Craft Assault over the side and down scrambling nets, there was a heavy swell which made it difficult. My flotilla circled round and off we set in pitch darkness for the beach we were supposed to assault. After about 15 minutes not only could I see no sign of the shore I could see no other craft anywhere. I was up in front near the coxswain and leaned over and looked at his compass, it was pointing east. I nudged him and said, "Are you sure it's OK?" "My God!" He spun his wheel, we were going in the dead wrong direction and would, given an hour or two, have arrived somewhere off the coast of Norway. We used live ammunition and had quite a few casualties from supporting fire and explosives during these rehearsals for 'breaking the Atlantic Wall.' The 4.2 inch mortars were usually held responsible if things went wrong, since although the bomb made a lovely bang it was a notoriously inaccurate weapon, and on one occasion fragments of bomb had to be extracted from a victim to prove or disprove it was the 4.2 inch mortars again – it was; I used to feel awfully sorry for them.... On another occasion I can remember taking the wrong direction and being trapped with a group of soldiers in an area being heavily shelled; we ran for it at a very fast speed.

Major Mike Ryan
Officer Commanding Support Company, 2nd Battalion Royal Warwickshire Regiment

Training for D-Day in the Moray Firth involved exercise landings. We found the condom, which had been issued for other purposes, most useful for keeping one's watch, cigarettes and tobacco dry. Its capacity was quite remarkable.

There was always a more light-hearted element for the men to enjoy, the Battalion War Diary records the men attending an 'all-ranks' dance on 3 March at the drill hall in Huntly, Aberdeenshire.

On 6 March 1944, the battalion adjutant, Captain Peter Batt was appointed General Staff Officer (GSO) III (Intelligence) and attached to 185th Brigade HQ. He was responsible, along with others, for coordinating intelligence, planning and training for the forthcoming landing. Peter had attended Rugby School and been employed as a chartered accountant in Coventry before the war, but having received high certification with the schools Combined Cadet Force, shortly after his enlistment was sent by the Royal Warwicks to Sandhurst, as part of the first wartime officer cadet training course where he was commissioned back into the regiment.

Captain Peter Batt
2nd Battalion Royal Warwickshire Regiment – GSOIII 185th Brigade HQ

> I was lucky enough to be in the right place at the right time and to have been selected for a most interesting job, a job shared by very few. I wasn't awfully good, and I certainly wasn't brave. I was just a little cog in a big machine.... I was ordered to a tiny village in Scotland to help with the organisation. We were told the invasion was to take place before 31 May and we had full details of the landing beaches, we knew exactly what was going to happen.... we had to arrange where to land, who to land and where, to find out where the German troops were, to sort out which of the French were on our side and which were not and we had to transport something like 120,000 men and 20,000 vehicles and to get them to the right beach and the right time and in the right order and making full use of the craft available to us.... [Monty] was determined that his old regiment, the Royal Warwicks, should be amongst the first to land in Normandy and I can tell you that we didn't thank him for the honour he gave us.

After courting for three years, Captain Batt became engaged to his future wife, Jean, amidst the build-up to invasion. The date was arranged for April 1944, a period of much activity and limited opportunity for leave, and not just for Peter, as Jean was a military nurse, subject to the same limitations. In a moment of daring pluck, Peter, posing as Brigadier K. P. Smith, telephoned the War Office to request a War Office Urgent Memorandum, for two weeks leave for the blushing bride. Fantastically, his plan worked, and the couple were happily married, with Lieutenant Phillip Healey, also of the Regiment, as their best man.

In the March edition of the Regiment's newsletter, *The Antelope*, the colonel of the regiment set the scene for their future endeavours:

Brigadier Clement Thurstan Tomes
The Royal Warwickshire Regiment

> We are on the eve of great events in which I feel sure the regiment will play a worthy part. So I will take the opportunity of sending all of you who will be employed in active operations my very best wishes. May good luck attend you wherever you may be and may your contribution to the success of our arms be a large one.

Following the successful landings in North Africa, Sicily and Italy, and the disastrous Dieppe Raid in August 1942, important lessons were learned and the proposal for a full scale invasion of France was approved. Eschewing the obvious target of the Pas-de-Calais, the Allies opted instead for the Normandy Coast, the easier route was obvious to the Allies and therefore also to the enemy. Defensive dispositions also made Normandy a more attractive proposition. Initially the invasion focused on three beaches Omaha, Gold and Juno with just four divisions, however after the appointment of Lieutenant General Dwight D. Eisenhower (Ike) as Supreme Commander and General Sir Bernard Law Montgomery KCB DSO, hero of El Alamein, as commander of the 21st Army, the original plan was deemed too restrictive and was increased by two additional beaches, the American Utah on the west flank and the British Sword Beach on the east flank against the River Orne, with the invasion now totalling eight divisions. The 3rd Division, including the 2nd Warwicks, was tasked with landing, taking and holding Sword Beach, with the subsequent move inland towards Caen, just 12km from the coast, which Monty had breezily told all before him would be in Allied hands by the end of the first day.

3

Build-Up

The largest armada in modern military history was about to set out, codenamed Operation Neptune, the seaborne element of Operation Overlord, the invasion of Northwest Europe. The initial assault would focus on two elements: firstly, drops inland behind enemy lines for both British and US airborne forces, by glider and parachute, followed by seaborne landings on the five separately targeted beachheads. In the west the US beaches of Utah near St-Mère-Église and Omaha at Verville, centrally was the first of two British beaches, Gold, near Arromanches, followed by the Canadian Juno Beach near Courseulles and Saint-Aubin-d'Arnquenay, and finally the easternmost sector, Sword Beach, the second British focal point. Each beach was broken down into independent sections, Sword splitting into sections Oboe, Peter, Queen and Roger. Queen section was the intended target for the British 3rd Division, this was split into three further sections, Green, White and Red. Queen Green was deemed inaccessible due to impassable offshore rocks and reefs, Queen White and Queen Red were identified as the landing points and it is Queen White in the Sword Beach Area that is the focus here, as it was on this roughly 800m stretch of coastline that the men of 2nd Warwicks came ashore.

The 3rd Division was under the command of Major General Tom Rennie DSO MBE, Rennie was an experienced combat officer having commanded a battalion in North Africa and been a brigade commander in the 51st Highland Division in Sicily. In 1943 Rennie returned to England to his promotion to Major General and command of 3rd Division, where we now find him. The division, like Queen Beach, was broken into three subsectors, brigades. Each of these brigades had its own allocated role to play. 9th Brigade was designated as assault brigade and the first to land, following up as intermediate brigade was the 185th, of which the 2nd Warwicks was a part, with 9th Brigade held as a reserve. Alongside the men of Warwickshire in the 185th were the 2nd Battalion Kings Shropshire Light Infantry (2nd KSLI) and 1st Battalion Royal Norfolk Regiment (1st Norfolks). 185th Brigade was commanded by Brigadier Kenneth Pearce Smith OBE, who had returned to the UK in 1943 after commanding a brigade in Malta. Commanding Officer of the 2nd Warwicks themselves was the imposing figure of Lieutenant Colonel Hugh Owen Seymour Herdon, HOS or Jumbo Herdon as he was affectionately known. Herdon had previously commanded 9th Battalion Royal Warwicks having first been posted as a Second Lieutenant in the regiment in 1923.[1]

On 9 April 1944, the regiment headed south to Lindfield in West Sussex, at Camp J8 in the grounds of the Paxhill Estate near Haywards Heath. Throughout April and May, the hard training continued with field firing exercises held at Kingsley Vale, street fighting drill at Lindon House, a visit to the School of Tank Technology to inspect heavy equipment and loading practice, culminating with the final dress rehearsal of Exercise Fabius on 4 May.

Lieutenant Adams had been commissioned into 14th Battalion Royal Warwickshire Regiment via Oxford University 164 OTC. On disbandment of the 14th Battalion in 1943, he was posted to the infantry training centre at Budbrooke Barracks in Warwick and in April 1944 finally posted to 8th Platoon, A Company, 2nd Battalion Royal Warwickshire Regiment as the battalion was engaged in final invasion training and preparation.

Lieutenant Kingston St John Adams
A Company, 2nd Battalion Royal Warwickshire Regiment

> I must admit my initial feelings were of being dropped in at the deep end, having to command a platoon of well-trained men who had nearly all experienced months of pre-invasion training and exercises up in Scotland and elsewhere and who were versed in all aspects of this type of warfare. I now joined in this training with them concentrating on laying and clearing mines and booby traps, street fighting, house clearing and field firing and all types of patrolling.
>
> On 2–5 May between Bognor and Littlehampton, Exercise Fabius, our dress rehearsal for the invasion took place. Due to bad weather the exercise (like the invasion itself) was postponed for 24 hours. The exercise consisted of a lot of marching, hurried recces and 'O' groups, attacks on various objectives around Arundel and at the end of the exercise marching back to our camp at Haywards Heath, about 30 miles. My Pl[atoon] actually cycled back on bicycles belonging to another company which had been given another task.

Eschewing the traditional regimental marching song, *Warwickshire Lads*, the men of the battalion were known to sing *My Mate Sylvest* while marching, sung in slightly more 'soldierly' language than the original 1908 song, *My Bruddha Sylvest*, although some of the older men might have preferred to sing more military songs. Private Dennis Pettitt would sing these marching songs to his children at the dinner table in later life, much to the annoyance of his wife as the language became more 'robust'.

It is worth noting that during Exercise Fabius, Brigadier Smith altered brigade orders, directing 2nd Warwicks and 1st Norfolks in a flanking advance beyond 2nd KSLI. In the confusion, this resulted in the three battalions of the brigade becoming separated, communication breaking down and the ultimate failure of the manoeuvre. Major

1 See Appendix II for 3rd Division Order of Battle.

General Rennie had witnessed this unfold and in his authoritative but unique style, quipped to Brigadier Smith "You won't let this happen on the day will you KP?"[2]

Finally, the battalion moved forward to the marshalling areas; all marching personnel were stationed at Camp J3, Firle Park near Lewes, with the fighting vehicles at Camp J4, Novington Manor near Plumpton and Battalion Headquarters vehicles heading for Camp J1, Middleton Manor near Westmeston.

Major T. L. Brock
HQ Company, 2nd Battalion Royal Warwickshire Regiment

> The organisation of these camps was excellent and everything was done for the comfort and amusement of the men. There were excellent NAAFI's, entertainment was provided by cinemas which operated almost continuously from dawn to dusk. Inter-platoon football matches were organised and very much enjoyed by all. Luckily the weather during this period was excellent and most unusual for the time of year. It was very encouraging to watch the almost continuous stream of aircraft of all types flying out over the Channel, and it made one realise the terrific scale of the operations about to commence.

The hard work was interspersed with 24 hour passes and an inspection from His Majesty King George VI on 22 May, which had followed the unfortunate defeat of the battalion football team, 3–2 (in extra time) at the Divisional Final in Portsmouth.

Brigadier Kenneth Pearce Smith OBE
Officer Commanding 185th Infantry Brigade

> I then received a message that His Majesty King George VI would be visiting the brigade. I selected a parade ground on an estate in which the Warwicks were encamped – and rang up Fortnum and Masons, requesting them to send by express a first-class tea for a 'very important personage'.
>
> His Majesty arrived, nearly half an hour late, and he was extremely apologetic and, pointing his finger at the 'brasshats,' said they were to blame. He inspected the parade.... His Majesty was most impressed.... Then on to a marquee where a sumptuous tea was laid out – sandwiches, cakes, meringues, et cetera and I asked His Majesty what he would like to start with, whereupon he said that he never ate at teatime but would love a cup of tea. After he had departed my staff and officers of the Warwicks, who were camped in the park, had a tremendous tuck in!

Sergeant Major Russell King
2nd Battalion Royal Warwickshire Regiment

> We had to stop blokes playing football eventually because there were that many blokes getting crocked playing, they were frightened they were going to be short of men I think. I remember quite a few lads getting ankles turned. Not serious injuries but enough to stop them marching anyway.... course that was about all

2 Stephen Fisher, *Sword Beach* (London: Bantam, 2024), p.279.

they had you know, there wasn't a great deal to do actually, there seemed to be a lot more physical training and football than there was anything else.

As the day drew near the battalion were confined to camp, along with all of the invasion force, from 0001 hours 26 May. Intense briefings were repeatedly given from 27 May. Thanks to men like Peter Batt, soldiers of all ranks were able to study maps, reconnaissance photographs and scale models of the invasion beaches to ensure they knew what the landing would look like, what they did not yet know was where they would be landed. All locations on maps had been given code words, with the main location indicated on the regiment's maps being POLAND. Although having been issued with French Francs and a basic French phrase book, they would at least know their intended country.

Captain Peter Batt
2nd Battalion Royal Warwickshire Regiment – GSOIII 185th Brigade HQ

As the weeks went by the pace got faster. We had large 3D models of all the landing beaches thanks to wonderful aerial photographs given to us by the RAF and the information we had from the French Resistance. Every little building, every hedge and every ditch was there to scale. And it was essential that as many as possible of the officers and troops saw these models, but of course they were only allowed to see them on the day before embarkation.

Private Dennis Pettitt
D Company, 2nd Battalion Royal Warwickshire Regiment

We were 10 or 11 to a tent and the day we were going, or the day before we thought we were going, discounting the weather of course, a sergeant come into the tent and says "Right, we've got our objective, we're going over to France, that's where it is, and he said our job is to liberate Poland." I said, "Just us few?" he said, "Don't be cheeky Pettitt. Poland is the code name, that's what it's called, Poland. So, whenever you get lost or you're in trouble, you're heading for Poland."

Lieutenant Kingston St John Adams
A Company, 2nd Battalion Royal Warwickshire Regiment

On 26 May the camp (J8) was sealed. During this period, we continued training and keeping fit and were occasionally entertained by ENSA. During one performance a certain Vic Oliver remarked on the life of a soldier as being 'rising with the lark and going to bed with a WREN!' On 31 May we moved down to Camp J3 near Newhaven. It was clear to us at this point the invasion was imminent.

Corporal Alec Graham Pugh
Carrier Platoon, 2nd Battalion, Royal Warwickshire Regiment

When the time came to move.... we drove by road down to just outside Gosport into a staging camp, the section commander, which in this case was myself, because we were a separate section of carriers going on our own, had to go and draw two days' emergency rations for his section. Which included: chocolate, oatmeal biscuits, compo tea and waterproof cigarettes, 20 cigarettes for a day and matches, waterproof matches and various other items.

Sergeant Dennis
2nd Battalion Royal Warwickshire Regiment

It was said that before D-Day everyone was briefed until they were sick to death of it. Previous reports of the steps taken by Monty to ensure that all the commanders knew the country they were going to fight in were not exaggerated.... They were amply repaid for all this trouble, and the nett result was that the enemy positions, even down to MG posts, were known, all artificial and natural features were familiar, and certain personnel even know the names of streets...

Major T. L. Brock
HQ Company, 2nd Battalion Royal Warwickshire Regiment

After the final preparations had been completed, every man received a payment of French Francs, as well as certain essential clothing.

A church service was held in the camp cinema; the sermon given by the padre, the Reverend J. Austin, will be long remembered by all those who attended this service. Finally, the commanding officer read out the Special Order of the Day from the Commander-in-Chief General Sir Bernard Law Montgomery KCB DSO.

The aim of the initial assault was to minimise the defensive structures in place and to keep the heads down of as many of the defenders as possible, ensuring the maximum time and space for the landing forces to establish a firm foothold on the beaches. Between Lion-sur-Mer and La Breche at Queen White sector in the Sword Beach Area, the latest Bigot maps (Bigot indicating a level of secrecy above Top Secret) showed just what was waiting for the invaders. An unappealing mix of obstacles; steel anti-tank 'hedgehogs,' rows of barbed wire, up to five rows of stakes many tipped with teller mines and even captured French shells, having had the detonators replaced to explode upon impact. It was essential that these obstacles should be neutralised or at the least avoided. Naval frogmen landed in advance, with Royal Engineers landing alongside the first assault parties in an attempt the clear the way for the following landing craft and troops.

Midshipman Rene Le Roy
Landing Craft Obstacle Clearance Unit

The Germans had put in tremendous defences on the beaches in rows and rows and with very Germanic five-yard spacing. There was an initial row of tree trunks with mines on. The next was criss-cross girders and next was another row. So, you had three rows of obstacles on basically all the beaches in Normandy. And teller mines were fitted on some of them or some of them had French 75mm shells with the nose cap changed to percussion caps for pressure, so you'd press on the shell

> and it would go off. Any landing craft coming in without seeing these obstacles could hit these fields.

Sword Beach represented the most formidable landing area of the operation, not least because the space available to land troops was limited by rock formations on the west between Lion-sur-Mer and Luc-sur-Mer and the eastern side of the sector was hindered by sandbanks. It was imperative that the incoming craft landed in the exact location required otherwise they would founder, the British and Canadian landing areas employed midget submarines, in position and waiting before the invasion, to guide craft to the correct location. These X Craft, were rejected by the Americans, resulting in great confusion and disorganisation on the western beaches.

The beach between Lion-sur-Mer and La Breche was a popular holiday destination, and the sea front was built up with residential properties, hotels and beautiful holiday homes, which made excellent defensive positions for the Germans. All the while the landing zone was threatened by the fortifications in Ouistreham, the naval base at Le Havre and the possibility of incoming defensive fire from the Merville Battery located on the eastern side of the Orne River estuary. In the landing area itself there were concrete pillboxes, anti-aircraft guns, anti-tank guns, flamethrowers, machine guns and mortars manned by the troops of the *10. Batallion* of *Infanterieregiment Nr 736*. Further inland were concrete strongholds known as *Wiedenstandnester*. These larger, fortified casements, generally containing two larger calibre 50mm or 75mm guns and up to 10 MG42 machine guns, were positioned to hold key inland routes and connecting the separate lines of defence. Their key locations facing the advance were WN21 (Trout) at Lion-sur-Mer, WN20 (Cod) at LaBreche, WN18 near Hermanville-la-Breche and WNI7 (Hillman) & WN16 (Morris) around Colleville-Plage.

Infanterieregiment Nr 736 formed part of the *Infanteriedivision Nr 716*, which defended the British and Canadian landing beaches and was one of 15 static divisions created specifically for anti-invasion and occupation duties. They had seen service in the Balkans in this capacity, but these were not the crack troops of the earlier war years. They were predominantly older men, with the fitter and younger troops having been drafted away from the division to serve in the East against the Russians. *Nr 716* was commanded by the then *Generalmajor* Wilhelm Richter consisted of *Infanterieregiment Nr 726* as well as *Infanterieregiment Nr 736* and *Artilleriebataillon Nr 1716* (formerly designated *Nr 656*). Recently added to his forces were two *Osttruppen* (eastern troops) battalions, East European, Russian and Ukrainian soldiers effectively often press ganged into service of the forces now occupying their homeland. The *Osttruppen Bataillon Nr 441* was seconded to *Infanterieregiment Nr 726* and *Osttruppen Bataillon Nr 642* to *Infanterieregiment Nr 736*. These troops were eyed with suspicion by many of their German comrades and one can easily understand why these men might not possess the dedication to the cause they were now forced to defend.

Bolstering the threat of German counter-attack was the unwanted presence of *21. Panzerdivision*. The division consisted of *Panzerregiment Nr 22* (formerly *Nr 100*), *Panzergenadierregiment Nr 125* and *Panzergenadierregiment Nr 192* (undersized with two battalions each, instead of the normal three), *Panzerartillerieregiment Nr 155*,

Panzerflugabwehrregiment Nr 305 (Panzer Anti-Aircraft Regiment), *Panzerpionierregiment Nr 220* and *Panzeraufklärungsbataillon Nr 21* (Panzer Reconnaissance Battalion). The *21. Panzerdivision not Panzerregiment Nr 21* was under the command of *Generalmajor* Edgar Feutinger, a favourite of Hitler after his support of the Nazi party in the early 1930s, but also a veteran of the siege of Leningrad where he was wounded. Under Feutinger's command as Commanding Officer of *Panzergenadierregiment Nr 192* was *Oberstleutnant* Rauch and of *Panzergenadierregiment Nr 125* the enigmatic *Major* Hans von Luck who had seen action in Poland and France in the early war years, followed by service in Russia and North Africa, before returning to France once more. This division was generally thought to have remained some 10–20 miles south of Caen, however elements of *Panzergenadierregimenter Nr 125* and *Nr 192* had already moved north of Caen and were in position around Lebisey and Blainville, armed with a mix of heavy machine guns, 75mm self-propelled guns and 20mm self-propelled flack guns. In addition, *Panzerjägerbataillon Nr 200* with 24 x 88mm anti-tank guns was in position to the north-west of Caen and four batteries of field and flak guns were deployed in the Périers-sur-Dan area and the high ground north of Caen. Following this all up within a day's march, were the fanatical *12. SS Panzerdivision 'Hitlerjugend'* near Lisieux and the *Panzer-Lehr-Division* near Chartres.

Much has been made about the inadequate and insufficient troops defending this sector of the Atlantic Wall, and while they most certainly were not the arrogant and confident troops of 1939–1940 who swept all before them, they did not need to be. The role of defender, in many ways is far simpler than that of the attacker. In its simplest terms, in a fortified position, each man simply needs to hold his position. To sit behind his weapon, whether machine gun, mortar, artillery piece or rifle and keep firing, no dramatic tactics or derring-do are necessary. Just keep firing at the enemy in front of you!

The 2nd Warwicks were given their mobilisation orders and were transported to the docks of Newhaven on 3 June, excitement grew, and all men drew two 24-hour ration packs. 'Mae West' life vests and waterproofed trousers were issued to the marching troops. But after only a few hours they began to disembark again. The process was repeated on 4 June, and there they waited not knowing if they would need to again leave and tramp back to the camp, or if they'd set sail, they'd geared themselves up for this once only to be disappointed, surely 'they' wouldn't do that to them again?

Captain Peter Batt
2nd Battalion Royal Warwickshire Regiment – GSOIII 185th Brigade HQ

> All was set for 5 June with H-Hour at 0725. And on 3 June in the early morning, I was duty officer at my headquarters and I received a phone call from the admiral in charge of the fleet, and it was simple and just: "Tell Kenneth that I can't have tea with him tomorrow!"[3] It was of course the signal to postpone D-Day. Some troops

3 Working so closely together, the intelligence team had resorted to first names, 'Kenneth' being Brigadier K. P. Smith of 185th Brigade.

were already loaded in cramped conditions in little flat nosed, flat bottomed boats which bounced about, and they really suffered.

Lieutenant Kingston St John Adams
A Company, 2nd Battalion Royal Warwickshire Regiment

On 3 June we embarked on our LCI 315. On 4th bad weather and storms in the Channel winds caused a 24 hrs delay. Had a very wet night and disembarked in the morning leaving our kit on board except for eating utensils and returned to Camp J3 for a meal and a short rest before re-embarking on our LCI after. It had been a miserable 24-hour delay for the weather to clear and on parading to embark one man was reported missing but was later found asleep in the corner of the NAAFI and not a deserter as had been feared. Sadly, he was one of the first to be killed on the next day.

Sergeant Major Russell King
2nd Battalion Royal Warwickshire Regiment

We weren't back in the training camp for more than a few hours and then we went back on the ship again, which was a bit off-putting. We were on and off, on and off, and people got a bit disconcerted. They thought it was just a bloody big flap like. Typical army.

The intended date for D-Day was Monday 5 June, but with exceptionally rough seas and poor weather, low cloud at 500ft and force-five winds the invasion was delayed. This time however, the troops would not disembark, they remained on board their transport ships, buffeted by the wind and the waves. The high winds and low cloud were the greater concern to General Eisenhower and his team, troops can land on the beaches in these conditions, but the essential air support could not operate, and they would not countenance the idea of landing without this. On the morning of 5 June, after much deliberation and meteorological advice, Eisenhower confirmed that the seaborne troops would set sail that night.

Sergeant Bob Barnett (Intelligence Sergeant)
B Company, 2nd Battalion Royal Warwickshire Regiment

We moved to a tented camp just behind Newhaven and then from there onto the boats and we'd just got on the boats when we had to come off again because the sea was too rough. We went back to these little tents for the night and then back down to the harbour the following day and I'll always remember Joe Dentith [16 Platoon D Company] one of the officers who later became the IO who was an actor by trade.... Joe conducted some community singing over the loud hailers on his boat in the harbour.

Captain Alastair JM Bannerman[4]
Officer Commanding Anti-Tank Platoon, 2nd Battalion Royal Warwickshire Regiment

> We had a visit from our battalion commander, who was in good form, and we were able to recognise our friends on boats moored in the vicinity. On the jeep of Sergeant Matthews in which I am going to land, the whole section has painted the names of their girls with a Cupid's heart in chalk. So, in order not to be left out I have added your name as well to the gallery and it now stands between the Doris of Lance Corporal Baker and the Vera of Sgt Matthews: Elisabeth Aear [Bannerman]. I know two officers very well whose wives expect a baby today and I can understand their feelings.

Lieutenant Kingston St John Adams
A Company, 2nd Battalion Royal Warwickshire Regiment

> The evening was spent in a wonderful singsong between members of the various boats in the harbour. The BBC had erected a mike and was broadcasting from one of the LCIs and various people started singing. This led to competition from the other boats and soon the whole harbour was ringing with songs. Laid down my bed on the upper deck tonight and just got settled down when a Scotch mist came down.

Not everybody agreed that the invasion would take place amidst the awful weather conditions, *Generalfeldmarschall* Rommel, 'the Desert Fox' himself, equipped with a pair of grey suede shoes made especially as a present, left Normandy on 5 June and had returned to Germany to meet with The Fuhrer and to celebrate his wife Lucie's birthday on 6 June – the shoes didn't fit....

***Major* Hans von Luck**
Panzergrenadierregiment Nr 125

> The evening of 5 June 1944 was unpleasant. Normandy was showing its bad side; during the day there had been rain and high winds.... The general weather conditions, worked out every day by naval meteorologists and passed on to us by division, gave the 'all clear' for 5 and 6 June. So, we did not anticipate any landings, for heavy seas, storms, and low lying clouds would make large-scale operations at sea and in the air impossible for our opponents.

4 Alastair Bannerman's father, Colonel John Arthur Murray Bannerman DSO, served as a Second Lieutenant with the 1st Battalion Royal Warwickshire Regiment during the Great War, alongside a young Captain Bernard Law Montgomery, where he was mentioned in dispatches three times and awarded the DSO. He was also commanding officer of 2nd Battalion between 1926 and 1930.

4

D-Day

Major TL Brock
HQ Company, 2nd Battalion Royal Warwickshire Regiment

> Accordingly, our force set sail that afternoon to join with the main force to the south of the Isle of Wight. It was an amazing voyage, the Channel appeared to be full of convoys, all in very orderly formation, but all sailing different courses. Towards evening the main force to which we were to join could be seen in the distance. It was an unforgettable sight, seeing the battleships, cruisers and other ships silhouetted against the setting sun.

Late in the evening of 5 June, Task Force S, the naval invasion fleet for Sword Beach, finally set sail from numerous ports across the south coast of England, for what the Battalion War Diary rather blandly describes as: 'An uneventful passage across the Channel in the direction of Normandy.'[1] Force S was broken down into three sections: S3 would transport the assault brigade (8th), S2 the intermediate brigade (185th, including the 2nd Warwicks) and S1 the reserve brigade (9th).

Captain Harry Illing
Officer Commanding A Company, 2nd Battalion Royal Warwickshire Regiment

> It was with tremendous relief after all our months of training and preparation that we embarked, amidst the cheers of the local W.R.N.S., the admonitions of a tired embarkation staff, and the hearty jollity of the BBC recording vans. Several of our men spoke over the air.
>
> Silently we left England, for so many for the first time, and so many for the last.

Private Dennis Pettitt
D Company, 2nd Battalion Royal Warwickshire Regiment

> … I think most, I can't speak for everybody, were looking forward to it in a sense of we knew we were on the verge of history, there had never been an invasion like it ever and the only people who had the quivers were the non-swimmers…. We set off from Newhaven, we set out very early…. the weather was very poor…

1 TNA WO 171/1387, '2nd Battalion, The Royal Warwickshire Regiment, War Diary,' 5 June 1944

Allocation of Battalion Officers – 6 June 1944

Battalion HQ	Lt. Col. H. O. S. Herdon – CO Maj. R. G. Kreyer – 2iC Capt. W. Pike – Adjutant Lt. P. W. F. Lamb – IO	**HQ Company**	Maj. T. L. Brock – OC Lt. J. R. Clarke – SO Lt. A. P. Roberts – TO Capt. S. J. Williams – QM Capt. J. H. T. Lawton (RAMC) – MO Capt. (Rev) J. Austin (RACD) – Padre Capt. J. Lee (RA) – FOB
A Company	Capt. H. Illing – OC	Capt. M. L. B. Hall – 2iC	
Platoon Commanders	Lt. K. St John Adams	Lt. J. Erskine	Lt. O. W. Jarvis
B Company	Maj. G. E. E. Ross – OC	Capt. G. F. J. Jerram – 2iC	
Platoon Commanders	Lt. A. Dockerty	Lt. D. A. Field	Lt. D. S. B. Roberts
C Company	Capt. W. T. Barratt – OC	Capt. R. W. Heath – 2iC	
Platoon Commanders	Lt. R. M. McCrory	Lt. R. Pratt	Lt. K. A. Taylor
D Company	Maj. T. G. Bundock – OC	Capt. C. O. Blakey – 2iC	
Platoon Commanders	Lt. C. Briggs	Lt. E. E. Dentith	Lt. V. C. Walton
Support Company	Maj. M. Ryan – OC		
Carrier Platoon	**Mortar Platoon**	**Anti-Tank Platoon**	**Assault Pioneer Platoon**
Capt. P. B. Waterworth – OC	Lt. P. M. Healey – OC	Capt. A. J. M. Bannerman – OC	Lt. A. G. Wilson
Lt. A. R. Allen – 2iC		Lt. J. Bindless – 2iC	

Lieutenant Kingston St John Adams
A Company, 2nd Battalion Royal Warwickshire Regiment

I had little time to think much about it, but in all our minds was the thought, would this be the last time we would see England? I still couldn't believe we were going into action at last, would be shot at, mortared, and would have every weapon the Germans possessed thrown at us to drive us away from their shores. Yet there was not one of us who was not proud to think he would be amongst the first to land on one of the greatest expeditions ever known in history.

There was no going back now, and just after midnight officers were authorised to open sealed envelopes that detailed the actual names and locations of their part of the invasion. Caen, came as a surprise to many of the troops, during the previous weeks there had been much speculation about their destination, with Dieppe, Calais, Le Havre and even Dunkirk being mooted. During the voyage they were passed by innumerable fleets of aircraft; bombers heading for Caen, the airborne division heading towards different drop zones and most telling were the Horsa gliders being towed overhead. At 0016 hours 6 June, six gliders under the command of Major John Howard landed near two bridges over the Caen Canal and Orne River, key bridges (later renamed Pegasus Bridge and Horsa Bridge) that represented the most direct route for German counter-attack on eastern bridgeheads about to be formed. If the Allies failed to take those bridges before the landing took place, *Panzerdivision Nr 21* would be able to race across, directly onto the flank of the troops landing on Sword Beach.

Captain Walter Pike
Adjutant, 2nd Battalion Royal Warwickshire Regiment

> It was a fantastic sight. The ocean was full of ships, the sky full of aircraft and morale was running high.

Captain Mike Ryan
Officer Commanding Support Company, 2nd Battalion, the Royal Warwickshire Regiment

> I've never forgotten the sea of masts.... you've never seen anything like it and never will again I don't suppose, most of the ships had these barrage balloons.

Captain Alastair J. M. Bannerman
Officer Commanding Anti-Tank Platoon, 2nd Battalion Royal Warwickshire Regiment

> I am writing still in the navigation room.... It is now 0300 hours.... It is rather light because the moon is shining, though heavy clouds cover her. One can see the row of small ships and of darker balloons silhouetted in front and behind us the grey sea. We are rolling a little, but the wind has subsided somewhat, thank heaven. The captain and his first officer are on the bridge. They make sure where we are and look for the coloured light which should guide us through one of our own minefields.

While Captain Bannerman tends towards the poetic, especially as his writings were intended for his wife's eyes, not all personnel were quite so comfortable, both he and Captain Illing mention their men suffering greatly from sick sickness: 'despite seasick pills, boiled sweets and cups of tea'[2] and the smell of the anti-tank platoon's quarters below deck being so overwhelming that Bannerman was forced to escape in search of fresh air on deck. But the reassuring presence of Captain the Reverend J. Austin,

2 H. C. Illing, *No Better Soldier* (Warwick: Privately Published, ND), p.14.

brought calm to many. A Methodist minister in uniform, he was a much sought-after man on the journey, for men searching for solace or reassurance in God or simply wanting someone to speak to.

Lieutenant Kingston St John Adams
A Company, 2nd Battalion Royal Warwickshire Regiment

> We set sail around 9 p.m. on the evening of 5 June. The crew were well known to most of the company having trained and practised with them on previous exercises.... At the appointed time around midnight the Company O Group began and we started opening and sorting out maps and other documents which for the first time showed proper place names instead of coded names such as POLAND for Caen and PORTUGAL for the Caen Canal. I had no fewer than 18 maps and papers to pack into kit bag and map case! It was difficult to concentrate on our own orders as the boat rocked and rolled on its crossing, but eventually we went off to brief our own section commanders who were billeted in the crew's cabin. Before turning in for the night I went up on deck and found even more ships had joined us including three battleships and six Destroyers, overhead bombers and fighters flew around and over us, giving most welcome protection from enemy interference.

The aerial attack of the defences along the Atlantic Wall commenced at 0300 hours, not just in Normandy but at multiple locations along the coastline in order to maximise confusion and uncertainly in where the landing would actually take place. The air force intervention was shortly followed by the navy; anchored 7 miles out to sea the shore bombardment fleet accompanying Force S began their bombardment of the Norman Coast at 0330 hours. HMS *Serapis*, HMS *Middleton* and the Polish destroyer ORP *Slazek* focusing on the beach defences around Queen White.

At 0510 hours the RAF provided low-flying aircraft to lay a defensive smoke screen for the incoming Task Force S. As well as providing visual protection for the landing craft, the smoke screen also enabled smaller craft, 24 LCTs specifically designed to hold rocket-firing armoured vehicles and self-propelled artillery units, to move closer to the shore to provide more localised fire. One negative of the smoke screen was that it allowed three torpedo boats (*T34*, *T35* & *T36*) from the German *5. Torpedobootsflottille* based at Le Havre to enter the landing zone in what was almost a suicide mission, sinking the Norwegian destroyer *Svenner* with the loss of 30 souls, before returning to their harbour.

Petty Officer John Abbott
Royal Navy – HMS *Largs*

> I was a young sick berth Petty Officer on HMS *Largs*, the senior sick berth rating aboard. She was an HQ ship, flagship of S Force, Rear Admiral Talbot flew his flag in her, and the beach that we were to take the 3rd British Infantry Division into was to become Sword Beach. Most of us had done it before, but this was the biggest yet and we felt our luck might run out after all the Mediterranean invasions. That Tuesday morning, we were chugging along steadily keeping station and the sea was

full of ships. It was very early, and I was up top with the Jaunty, somebody or something was making smoke, I think it was to starboard of us. We both looked, and looked again, and there were two tin fish heading straight for us. What a panic, the lookouts were going mad, somehow the old *Largs* went astern, and those two fish whizzed across our bows slap into the Norwegian destroyer *Svenner*, stationed on our port side. She broke in two halves and went under, making a 'V'. It was awful, and under orders no one stopped for survivors

Lieutenant Kingston St John Adams
A Company, 2nd Battalion Royal Warwickshire Regiment

The officers were in a cabin, but my platoon was down in the bowels of the ship and the atmosphere was awful.... The ship was rocking and rolling and a good number of them were very ill. Some people were being sick in our cabin too, and I had to go into the engine room to get some sleep.

At 0530 hours men began to emerge on the deck of their transport craft to begin the arduous task of boarding the smaller and lighter landing craft. 2nd Warwicks were well acquainted with the crew of their LCI, they had worked with the same crews through Exercise Fabius, and it was reassuring to have those same faces with them for the real thing. Then with dawn upon them, the LCIs embarked towards land. First ashore on Queen White at H-Hour minus 10 minutes, were the oft forgotten 5th Assault Regiment Royal Engineers and the now famous 'swimming tanks'; 40 Sherman Duplex Drive tanks of A & B Squadrons, 13th/18th Hussars were launched and having launched closer to shore than planned almost all arrived, although some became swamped as the tide rose, with 23 surviving the assault. It was believed that only one company of *Infanterieregiment Nr 736* would be facing the troops landing on Sword Beach, the reality was that both *1.* & *2. Bataillons* of the *Regiment* were facing the landing on this section of coastline, making it a far more formidable prospect. *3. Bataillon, Infanterieregiment Nr 736* was held in reserve inland and *Ostbataillon Nr 642* was dispersed further inland towards the Orne.

At H-Hour, 0725, the main assault forces touched down; the 1st Battalion South Lancashire Regiment on Queen White and 2nd Battalion East Yorkshire Regiment on Queen Red. The infantry assault companies were supported by a host of armour; Sherman flail tanks of the 22nd Dragoons, elements of A Squadron, Westminster Dragoons and the 77th Assault Squadron Royal Engineers with a selection of their Assault Vehicle Royal Engineers (AVRE), either with a 230mm petard spigot mortar ('flying dustbin'), carrying fascines,[3] or with a small box girder bridge, or laying mats to assist the vehicles following, and armoured D7 bulldozers to clear paths. Churchill Crocodiles[4] with their terrifying flamethrower are usually included in this list of 'Hobart's Funnies,' there were however no Crocodiles deployed on 6 June on Sword Beach, they would follow in later

3 A bundle of palings, carried on an AVRE and dropped into anti-tank ditches to enable tanks to cross.

4 Flamethrower tank

waves of the assault.[5] H-Hour had been set almost an hour after the Americans at Utah & Omaha to take best advantage of the low tide. The intention was to land the troops below the beach obstacles allowing the infantry to advance up the beach using them as cover, however due to the weather, the tide was higher than usual, meaning that the landing craft arrived as the obstacles were almost completely submerged, subjecting the unwieldy craft to manoeuvring round them, many craft would be damaged or sunk because of this.

As the assault troops set down on the sand, the soldiers of the intermediate brigade began their own passage to shore. The run in was rough, not helped by the LCIs' flat bottoms, but the men were poised and focused ahead, Captain Illing searching for and finding the gable ended house he'd seen so many times in photographs. As land came into sight, the deep roar of the navy's gunfire was heard and felt by all, and they headed down the cleared channels in the minefield. At H+60 the first party of 2nd Warwicks, from LCI 228 set foot on Norman sand. Major Mike Ryan,[6] OC Support Company, acting as Unit Landing Officer and a small team consisting of one NCO from each company in the battalion, were to pave the way for the four rifle companies and battalion headquarters due to land shortly.

Major Mike Ryan
Officer Commanding Support Company, 2nd Battalion Royal Warwickshire Regiment

> In June 1944, I was OC Support Company in the 2nd Battalion, the Royal Warwickshire Regiment, 185 Infantry Brigade, 3rd British Infantry Division. The other two battalions in the brigade were the 1st Royal Norfolk Regiment and the 2nd KSLI. The division's task was to land on Sword Beach and secure the eastern flank and push on to Caen.
>
> I was, for the day, Unit Landing Officer. I landed just after 0730 with the 1st Bn. Suffolk Regiment, 8th Infantry Bde. I had a guide from each Company with the task of reconnoitring a suitable assembly area for the 2nd Battalion, their guides to meet them as they landed and show them the way.

Lieutenant Kingston St John Adams
A Company, 2nd Battalion Royal Warwickshire Regiment

> We put on our mackintosh waders over all our equipment, but Harry [Captain Illing] decided to leave them behind after all, so we proceeded to struggle out of them again. We were going full speed for the shore now, and through our binoculars could see what was left of our objectives after the terrific hammering of the RAF. All the men were fully dressed and waiting in the correct order below decks ready to come up. I went down and wished them all good luck.

5 As with midget submarines, American forces rejected the use of AVREs on Utah and Omaha beach. The lack of this support greatly hampered the ability of the US soldiers trying to create exits from Omaha beach.

6 *The Antelope, The Journal of The Royal Warwickshire Regiment.* (2004 Edition).

At this point the three LCIs fanned out into line for the final run in, all the while with the whipping sound of missiles passing overhead from the artillery and machine-gun posts ashore. 539 men, with 113 bicycles, landed on time at 0955 hours (H+150) in three LCIs. Supporting these soldiers were the 105mm howitzers of the M7 Priest self-propelled guns of 7th Field Regiments Royal Artillery, the 3-inch anti-tank guns of the M10 Wolverine SPs of 20th Anti-Tank Regiment RA, L Section Divisional Signals of the Royal Signals Regiment with their No.22 sets and elements of 223rd Field Ambulance Company RAMC and 17th & 253rd Field Companies Royal Engineers.

Peter Batt and his batman, Private George Hollins, representing HQ 185th Infantry Brigade landed at the same time. As a side note, some people simply view an officer's batman as a servant, but working so close together in such trying circumstances, in many instances a very close bond was formed between the two men. Peter and George remained friends until their dying days, and their respective widows remained in contact until their deaths.

It was perhaps fortunate that Captain Illing instructed his men to remove the waders, with the depth of water the battalion disembarked into, the waders would have immediately filled with water, at best making it more difficult to move, at worst causing troops to slip below the water altogether.

Captain Harry Illing
A Company, 2nd Battalion Royal Warwickshire Regiment

> We could see spouts of water shoot up as enemy bombs and shells fell into the sea and small clouds of black and white smoke rise up as the enemy fire came down on the beaches. The naval gunfire had lifted to targets behind, but our planes swept overhead.... Nothing hit our craft as we raced in, but other companies were not so lucky.

Uncertain of the reception the assault brigade had received, they headed towards the shore. LCI 315[7] transporting Captain Illing's A Company was unscathed, the taller men like Lieutenant 'Tiny' Adams at over 6 feet tall managed to wade ashore relatively well, but the shorter men found it harder as the waves continued to pound them as they tried to keep their footing. LCIs 314 and 316 suffered during the landing, Captain W. T. Barratt's C Company LCI hit a mine as it beached, ammunition boxes exploded and fell, killing the signals sergeant on board. B Company's LCI under Major G. E. E. Ross with Major Bundock, sections of D Company and the CO on board, hit a mine off its bow and was struck three times by German artillery fire before the men could disembark. With both ramps damaged in order to get the men off, they had to pull alongside a stationary LCT from the assault wave, scrambling over onto that before then finally wading to the shore. Struggling ashore, they were not a little surprised by the sight of

7 Lieutenant Kingston St John Adams, Personal account of the Normandy Landings (Unpublished, date unknown).

an incredibly brave French girl,[8] most likely 18-year-old Jacqueline Noel,[9] who had gone down to the beach that morning in search of a missing bathing costume and was now helping wounded soldiers from the shallows.

Lieutenant Kingston St John Adams
A Company, 2nd Battalion Royal Warwickshire Regiment

> Finally, 'H' hour…. arrived and we disembarked, one ramp was dropped into the sea causing a temporary delay as soldiers had to use the other ramp to get off the boat but eventually we started to wade ashore. The water was deeper than we thought and some of the shorter men found the sea up to their waists and must have had a difficult time getting ashore carrying their weapons and equipment weighing up to a 100lbs in some cases.

Private John Pettifer
Signalman 2nd Battalion, the Royal Warwickshire Regiment

> As we were coming in we got hit by a shell, it pitched us up onto a landing craft that had already landed. So we climbed off ours, onto theirs and had a dry landing.

Private Dennis Pettitt
D Company, 2nd Battalion Royal Warwickshire Regiment

> It was Lion-sur-Mer, there was a three or four storey building, that was not only the point of our centre target, it was also reinforced by the Germans who fired at us from it. And of course we were fired at by shells from Merville Battery[10] at Ouistreham, because they could fire straight across the beach, and we were hit four times, the first time was one of the ramps was hit and shot away and the sailor…. shouted down "Port ramp shot away, all troops use the starboard ramp." Ok, starboard, which is the starboard bloody ramp, so then, you won't believe this, two or three minutes later BANG, [and the sailor said] "Starboard ramp shot away, I don't know what the bloody hell you're going to do now!" Thanks very much, … then we had an almighty wallop and he shouts down, "All troops on deck. All your bikes have gone." [We had] folding bikes so that we could race to Caen and take Caen before the panzers got there. These generals, honestly, bloody generals…. Then another bang, a fourth time, this was all from Merville, and we were on fire at the back, so we had to lash onto the Norfolks' boat…. we had to transfer very gingerly from there to there without getting your feet trapped between the two boats, and then get off down their ramps…. We had to go up the sandy beach right through to a lane that ran across the top…. Bren Gun Carriers, dead bodies, first time I'd ever seen a naked body, stretched out, obviously burnt his clothing off whoever he was the poor bugger…

8 Max Hastings, *Overlord* (London: Michael Joseph Limited, 1984), p.123.
9 Jonathan Mayo, *D-Day Minute by Minute* (London: Short Books, 2014), p.209.
10 Whist this was Dennis's perceived experience, we do know that the Merville Battery had been silenced by this time. The incoming artillery fire most likely came from the 75mm guns of the COD strong point, sited where Queen Red & White beaches meet.

Major Mike Ryan
Officer Commanding Support Company, 2nd Battalion Royal Warwickshire Regiment

> We wore assault jerkins rather than webbing equipment. These were made of canvas with pockets for everything, pack, haversack, water bottle, and ammunition. We carried 150 rounds each, two days' hard rations and spare socks, underclothing etc. Fairly heavily laden, rifle as well, we had to land with our belt and epaulettes completely undone because, if we fell in deep water, we could slip it off and avoid drowning! In addition to all this one of our companies waded ashore carrying bicycles! The planners must have been carried away. The idea was that this company should ride behind a squadron of tanks and capture the southern exits from Caen. In the event a number of bicycles were left in the sea.

Made in Birmingham by the small-arms manufacturer BSA, the folding airborne bicycles issued to troops all along the beach, were an inconvenience to say the least. Many were 'lost' immediately as the troops waded ashore, many more fell to the wayside; in some cases, troops of many regiments left their bicycles in the path of an oncoming tank whence they would be crushed beyond use, so as to rid themselves of the encumbrance.

Captain Harry Illing
Officer Commanding A Company, 2nd Battalion Royal Warwickshire Regiment

> In we drew to the shore, to see burning craft and to hear the crump of mortars and crack of bullets, for many, the first enemy fire. Bill Barratt's ship received a hit, but fortunately with only a few casualties. Then a gentle shock as we struck the coast of Normandy. One of our ramps broke; quick shout of orders as we piled off to starboard…

Lieutenant Kingston St John Adams
A Company, 2nd Battalion Royal Warwickshire Regiment

> By the time we reached the beaches most of the opposition had been heavily strafed from the air and we were able to get to our assembly area with few causalities, but soon after digging in there, we had our first real battle inoculation from German machine gunners, but luckily did not lose many.

Captain Peter Batt
2nd Battalion Royal Warwickshire Regiment – GSOIII 185th Brigade HQ

> … I was cluttered up with bulky radio sets ready for use as soon as we landed and at dawn we were there; chaos, noise, sinking boats, dead men, wounded men crying out, drowned men, awful minefields. Down the scrambling nets we went into one of these dear little flat bottomed boats called an LCT and we waded ashore picking our way through the casualties dodging the snipers, who were having a field day.

Captain Harry Illing
A Company, 2nd Battalion Royal Warwickshire Regiment

> We heard the whining noises more often now; this we knew was enemy fire, our first. We were very keyed up – unnaturally calm, with thumping chests and a deep sinking feeling in our stomachs. At last we touched the beach. Down went the ramps and ashore we stumbled, lugging our kits through the last few yards of shallow sea, up breathless and anxious on to the sandy beach. Up the beach we hurried towards the 'gable-end house' – it seemed like an old friend by now. Down we flopped – we were ashore, then up again to get clear of the beach and under cover. Nobody much seemed hurt, we most of us seemed to be there. We were on French soil. We had made the landing anyway.

Under mortar and sniper fire from the French homes along the promenade there was a great deal of confusion, but while a small number of casualties were inflicted the majority of the battalion made it ashore. The narrow strip of beach was gridlocked with damaged equipment, armoured fighting vehicles and men crammed even more tightly together by an extraordinarily high tide which had rendered the beach less than 30m deep. The leading brigade had begun their move inland, but well sited exits were still limited as 2nd Warwicks took cover on the beach. Captain Bannerman was able to source a D7 bulldozer to aid his team as they began to queue to leave the beaches.[11] Understandably the heaviest fighting had confronted the assault wave, but the beach was not clear as the battalion landed and isolated machine-gun posts and snipers continued to harass the troops on the beach and had to be dealt with piece by piece.

Lieutenant Kingston St John Adams
A Company, 2nd Battalion Royal Warwickshire Regiment

> Though the beach was meant to be clear there were still a few snipers blazing away. One in particular I remember firing away from the top of a ruined house – we took shelter behind a Sherman tank which had been knocked out and in the next moment the house which was firing blew up with a round from an Oerlikon.[12]

The battalion advanced up the beach, clambering over a small sea wall and crossing a small railway line. Making their way from the beaches towards the houses this was the first time that many of the troops had seen a dead body, with both German and British soldiers lying around them in the contorted manner in which they fell, an image that many of those present would never forget. As they headed along a lane towards a cross-road, explosions and machine-gun fire were continuous, but at least for now the men were not under direct fire.

11 Alastair Bannerman, *If I Don't Come Home, Letters from D-Day* (London: ITV Ventures, eBook, 2024), p.56.
12 Oerlikon: 20mm Anti-Aircraft Cannon, often used in an anti-infantry role.

Major Mike Ryan
Officer Commanding Support Company, 2nd Battalion Royal Warwickshire Regiment

> It (the battalion) had a certain amount of difficulty. Disembarkation from LCIs was by steps down either side of the bow and some had been damaged by shell fire.
>
> We met them and diverted them on to the exits from the beach. My guides left with their own companies and I was left to wait for mine.
>
> I watched 9th Infantry Brigade come ashore. KOSBs had a piper in the bows of each LCI. It was still a bit noisy to hear and appreciate this Scottish wail.

At 1125 hours (H+240) 101 Support Company troops and 25 vehicles, with Major Ryan waiting on the beach, followed ashore from three LCTs. Universal Carriers, halftracks, motorcycles, six of Captain Bannerman's 6-pdr anti-tank guns, and seven mortar carriers led by Lieutenant Philip Healey, who were accompanied by 41st Anti-Tank Battery RA, 15th Field Park Company Royal Engineers, 25 members of the 2nd Battalion The Middlesex Regiment in five carriers providing divisional machine gun and mortar support, two cars of the 3rd Battalion Reconnaissance Regiment (Royal Northumberland Fusiliers), and HQ 241st Provost Company.

Captain Harry Illing
Officer Commanding A Company, 2nd Battalion Royal Warwickshire Regiment

> Our next task was to get forward to our objective – the cemetery. We advanced along the road – not a soul in sight. Explosions and shots were going off in every direction. The hubbub was enormous, but no fire seemed to be directed particularly at us. As we turned off the road to cut across to our objective, out of the corner house popped a Frenchman. He looked typically and unmistakably French, even to wearing a beret and spectacles and wore the words F.F.I. on his armband. "Mine, Mine," he shouted, pointing to our intended route across the fields. We ploughed on with mine detectors to the fore, but no mine exploded, and soon we reached the cemetery and started digging. It all seemed very easy – only a few chaps had been hurt. There was plenty of fire about, but we hadn't been shot up badly.

The battalion (four companies and Battalion HQ) had made it to the assembly point in the cemetery between Lion-Sur Mer and Hermanville-sur-Mer, but after a very short period of rest, the cemetery soon erupted as A & C companies received incoming enemy fire. Firstly, snipers and then heavier machine-gun fire from *3. Kompanie, Osttruppenbataillon Nr 632* being directed at them from German positions to the west. Some dozen casualties were suffered at this point with Lieutenant Richard Pratt from C Company being shot twice – in the knee and leg.

Sergeant Major Russell King
C Company, 2nd Battalion Royal Warwickshire Regiment

> I always remember going down the ramp, there was a hell of a turmoil all over the bloody place.... I remember going up the beach, there was a little sea wall, maybe

> about four or five-foot-high, I remember passing this Priest tank, one of these self-propelled guns on the beach.... there was a lot of mortar fire and shell fire, a terrible lot of shell fire, mortar fire rather, and small arms of course. But the small-arms fire seemed to be coming from this big gabled end house I seem to remember.... Our forming up place of all places was the cemetery.
>
> We lost a few [men], didn't seem to lose many mind, the first one that I saw, he was an officer, he was in my company, a Lieutenant, Pratt. Lieutenant Pratt.... he was lying halfway across the road as we went down the railway track towards this cemetery.
>
> I remember going in this cemetery, and the Germans had a fixed line on the cemetery gates.... with a heavy machine gun and the bloody bullets were ricocheting off the gravestones. Hell of a lot of small-arms fire.

Lieutenant Kingston St John Adams
A Company, 2nd Battalion Royal Warwickshire Regiment

> The platoon was round me in trenches.... unfortunately, C Company got a lot of casualties as they had not dug in – what a lesson! Private Cross was our only casualty, with a bullet in his wrist. He was standing a yard from me when they had first opened up. Poor old Dicky Pratt was hit in both legs – our first officer casualty. Harry got orders to me to withdraw into the cemetery, but the only entrance was well and truly covered by the Boche, so we put down a smokescreen and section by section raced for the open gap. Luckily we managed it.

Captain Harry Illing
Officer Commanding A Company, 2nd Battalion Royal Warwickshire Regiment

> It seemed peaceful enough at the cemetery for about 10 minutes, and then we began to realise there really were some enemy. First snipers started, and then fairly heavy machine-gun fire came down. Within a few moments movement was almost impossible. Several men were soon hit. There was nothing to do but lie low and dig in as best we could. Our sniper team went forward through the corn to tackle their enemy counterparts. They got one German in a tree and another in some bushes, but soon one was shot through the knee. Then there came an order to move, and we wormed our way back under cover of our own smoke and fire, and under heavy enemy fire. We left the cemetery some dozen fewer than when we got there – it was our first real aperitif for battle.

Remarkably, the ever resourceful Captain Illing had acquired from sources unknown, a horse, so that he was able to ride between positions ensuring he kept in constant contact with his forward troops.[13]

As if to reinforce the danger of the snipers, one of Captain Illing's own snipers, Private Robinson returned to his section with three bullet holes in the stock of his rifle.

13 Harry Illing, Letter dated 18 June 1944.

Private Dennis Pettitt
D Company, 2nd Battalion Royal Warwickshire Regiment

Topper Brown... he was our battalion sniper! One because he was a bloody good shot and secondly because he appeared to have no fear. He did mind you, but everybody thought he was fearless. And the first time he came to my notice was on D-Day and we were sending out patrols, probing as they called it, and this one patrol got somebody killed and others wounded from a sniper's nest. They couldn't get near this sniper nest; they knew where it was but couldn't get near it because the snipers were so accurate. So Topper Brown said to Major Bundock, let me have a go. So, half an hour later... you heard this crack, I said that's a .303, that's Topper and then we heard a bbrrrrrm [German machine gun], I thought that's the end of Brown. A few minutes later, another .303. He'd wiped out the sniper nest.... on his own, and to cap it all a Canadian pilot had bailed out and he'd come down behind German lines. And what happened, down the road comes two German soldiers, privates, the Canadian pilot and Brown (whistling) he'd captured and brought them here, I thought bloody marvellous, nobody ever got a mention for that.

Major Mike Ryan
Officer Commanding Support Company, 2nd Battalion Royal Warwickshire Regiment

About 12 noon vehicles started to come ashore and were smartly hustled off the beach. By now we had three gaps in the minefield. Each vehicle carried, in addition to its normal load, a case or two of tinned compo rations, tins of self-heating soup and coffee which were dropped and formed into a ration dump.

The coffee and soup were delicious, heated by applying a cigarette to the element in the lid. I have always been surprised that this was not developed commercially. To add to this luxury, we had bread for breakfast before landing. On all previous exercises it was army biscuits.

At about 1400 hrs Support Company, having landed and organised, set off to join the battalion and we caught up with it near Hermanville.

The original plan was for the brigade to advance along the line Hermanville – Beuville – Lebisey – Caen. This route would be cleared by 2nd KSLI riding with the Shermans of the Staffordshire Yeomanry, with 2nd Warwicks and 1st Norfolks mopping up in their wake on the right and left respectively. But with armour stuck on the beach still and with the heavily defended German strongpoints of WD16 (Morris) and WD17 (Hillman) to the south of Hermanville, and Colleville being held against the advancing forces; mirroring his decision during Exercise Fabius, Brigadier Smith made an on the spot change of plan, again splitting his battalions. After a reorganisation, and an all-important brew up in Hermanville, the 2nd Warwicks were diverted passed Hermanville and Colleville, heading south-east towards Bénouville via Saint-Aubin-d'Arnquenay led by B Company, suppressing the remaining elements of the 736th Grenadier Regiment trying to delay the advance.

Captain Harry Illing
Officer Commanding A Company, 2nd Battalion Royal Warwickshire Regiment

The plan had been changed. The Germans were trying to break across the River Orne from the east. We were to go east and stop them. We assembled behind the cemetery under cover and then set off on a fast march to Hermanville. Here the Battalion reassembled, and the companies saw each other for the first time since leaving England.

Brigadier Kenneth Pearce-Smith OBE
Officer Commanding 185th Infantry Brigade

I established my HQ at the gates of Hermanville Town Hall, and my battalions reported their arrival at their forming up areas. Warwicks on the right, Norfolks on the left and the KSLI ahead on the Hermanville – Caen road, ready for their advance. The only other unit of my brigade that so far had got through the beach chaos was the 7th Field Regiment, RA, and for a short while was in the front line.

Meanwhile I received information that 21st Panzer Division was advancing west of Caen but there were no signs of my Staffordshire Yeomanry having got through the congestion on the beach and remembering the case of a brigade commander, one of whose battalions was decimated because he had sent them forward without anti-tank support, I was not going to send either KSLI or the Warwicks into a tank trap. I accordingly ordered Colonel Herdon to move over to the other flank and to advance by the River Orne road.

I had decided that, in any case, the Warwicks would be better placed on the left flank. Unfortunately, the Staffordshires were not at full strength, some of their tanks having been diverted to the Hillman battle. Meanwhile, and unknown to me, 9th Brigade was not following up on my right as planned, but had been diverted to Hillman and Pegasus area, and Jim Cunningham [Brigadier J. G. Cunningham, OC 9th Brigade] himself had been severely wounded. On my left flank the Warwicks were continuing their advance along the Orne Road, meeting increasing resistance.

Captain Bannerman appears to be one of the few Allied soldiers across the entire Normandy front to record interference from the Luftwaffe this day: 'A few Junkers 88 bombed the villages…. Two Messerschmitts flew over us, firing at our vehicles.'[14] On the outskirts of Bénouville the battalion came under small-arms fire, upon which Captains Illing's A Company were required to launch an attack in order to force passage through to the bridges over the Caen Canal and Orne River currently held by 6th Airborne Division, including Major John Howard's 2nd Battalion Ox & Bucks Light Infantry.

14 Alastair Bannerman, *If I Don't Come Home, Letters from D-Day* (London: ITV Ventures, eBook, 2024), p.56.

Lieutenant Kingston St John Adams
A Company, 2nd Battalion Royal Warwickshire Regiment

> We had a series of villages to clear on the way, which were mostly full of enemy snipers, rather than being held in strength. These caused us a lot of trouble all the time, as they were so difficult to find and clear out.

The constant harassment from snipers, and their preference to target men of rank, had started to cause many NCOs in particular to remove the stripes from their arms, so as to appear to be a private soldier to the enemy.

Captain Harry Illing
Officer Commanding A Company, 2nd Battalion Royal Warwickshire Regiment

> Orders came to launch an attack on Benouville. A hasty plan was made, and we formed up behind some farm buildings and a long high wall. Two lone Germans ran towards us unaware of our presence. As we moved into view, the Germans dived into a large hedge for cover, but before they could open fire a very willing Sten gunner shot them neatly in a pair from over the hedge.

With reinforcements arriving by glider, the defenders of Bénouville were distracted long enough for the assault to be successful, the gliders of 6th Airlanding Brigade landed in and around the position held by the 2nd Warwicks. As inspiring as the arrival of the gliders was, the battalion were not aware of this stage in the plan, and their delight soon turned to shock as the gliders descended amongst them. Landing so close in fact that two B Company signallers, with headphones on, concentrating on their No.18 sets were killed when one glider overshot and inadvertently landed directly on their position. It wasn't just the gliders that needed to be avoided, as the Halifaxs towing the gliders released their load, they also discarded the heavy tow ropes, which cascaded down onto the troops positioned below them. The keyed up airborne troops aboard the gliders, in many cases sprang from their mounts firing at an enemy that hadn't appeared, causing more casualties amongst the troops. When they arrived, Bénouville was still occupied, but the remaining defenders, particularly 'those ever cunning snipers' were soon dispatched.[15]

Lieutenant Kingston St John Adams
A Company, 2nd Battalion Royal Warwickshire Regiment

> My recollection of the fighting in Benouville was the company forming up for the attack on the village with two platoons forward and mine in reserve. We had a rather exposed route to the village across open fields with a small ravine between.
>
> My platoon encountered two German officers taking cover in a ditch beside our route, they were probably on some form of recce but they never got back to report their observations!

15 H. C. Illing, *No Better Soldier* (Warwick: Privately Published, ND), p.16.

> As the platoon entered the village it was clear that it had been hit severely by air raids previously and there was not much opposition to clear after the leading platoons had been through. But unfortunately a few snipers were still around to cause us a few casualties…

The assault was undertaken by Tiny Adams' platoon, in his diary he noted at the time that is was 'rather a shambles.'[16] Adams' batman was killed during the attack as they came under concentrated sniper fire.

Lieutenant Kingston St John Adams
A Company, 2nd Battalion Royal Warwickshire Regiment

> He was on the other side of the road from me at the time, and was shot in the head and died very quickly, which was merciful. He was a grand lad and I was awfully sad to lose him – poor chap…
>
> We passed a burning British tank which lit up the place for yards around. We were warned it was full of high explosive ammo and might blow up any minute, but nothing happened, and I remember thinking what a trifling worry it was, compared to all the others that we had gone through that day, and yet how scared we would have probably been had we passed the same thing on an exercise in England.

As part of the ever changing picture, the advance of 2nd East Yorks had been delayed just south of Ouistreham at WN12, the strongpoint codenamed Daimler by the Allies. The 2nd Warwicks was therefore required to relieve the airborne forces in Bénouville and provide protection for the two captured bridges. So, somewhat dismayed by the defensive perimeter they were expected to maintain, D Company remained in Bénouville. For many of us, primarily due to the film *The Longest Day* (admittedly the author's all-time favourite film) the overriding image of the bridges is Lord Lovat relieving Major John Howard, portrayed by Richard Todd, on the Caen Canal bridge, and this turn of events flies on the face of this – the reality is that Lovat's men were not the first beach landing troops to reach Major Howard! Assault Engineers and elements of the 2nd East Yorks had already achieved this. And secondly they did not actively relieve Howard's beleaguered men. The commandos absolutely arrived at the bridges and with Bill Millin's pipes playing, but they continued on their own mission.

Leutnant Hans Hoeller of *8. Kompanie* with eight 75mm SPs under *Oberleutnant* Braatz, had been in position around Lebisey Wood before the invasion, but having been woken early by his runner with warning of parachutists landing, now found themselves on the southern outskirts of Bénouville. Much of *21. Panzerdivision* were inexperienced after the *Afrika Korps* was essentially destroyed in Tunisia, however Hoeller was an exception, having served with 15. *Panzerdivision* in North Africa, and being evacuated before capitulation with a number of serious bullet wounds.

16 Andrew Williams, *D-Day to Berlin* (London: Hodder & Stoughton, 2004) p.68.

***Leutnant* Hans Hoeller**
8. Kompanie, 2. Bataillon, Panzergenadierregiment Nr 192

In front of us, in the Benouville houses to the left, everything was quiet. Straight ahead at the bridge there was one mortar hit after another. *Feldwebel* Tanner was making a good job of it. The British.... were probably cussing our mortars; after all, they had been under their fire the whole day. Waving my hand, I ordered the SPG to the front, positioning the grenadiers to safeguard both of its flanks. I wanted to prevent any surprise flanking attacks...

Private Dennis Pettitt
D Company, 2nd Battalion Royal Warwickshire Regiment

The battalion was split up because of the problem at Pegasus Bridge.... My company, D company, was detailed off to go to Benouville. And we had to fight our way to relieve the paras, who were under fire from the German counter-attack, so we had to help them out.

You had to keep your head down from the chateau, the chateau of course had got a direct line of fire onto the bridge and the Germans had a big sniper group on the roof of the chateau and it was causing a problem, so we sent for an RAF Typhoon.... he didn't have much trouble finding the target and this Typhoon came straight down the canal, he let off two rockets, zoom zoom, and the roof, half of it, disappeared and that was the end of the German sniper group.

When we arrived in the afternoon of D-Day I went into Madame Gondree's shop, the café, to buy a glass of wine and I think I must have been one of the first people in Europe from the British forces who actually had a glass of wine.

Private Ted Bedford
D Company, 2nd Battalion Royal Warwickshire Regiment

As we were approaching Benouville on 6 June we were sent to assist the airborne company which had landed in gliders after midnight on June 5/6, and attacked the German defences at Pegasus Bridge over the canal which runs parallel to the River Orne.

We spent some hours rooting out German snipers until well after midnight, I had been detailed to guard the rear and look out for an expected counter-attack. After a few hours none of my comrades had returned as arranged, so I went to the airborne position to enquire. After I was challenged I was informed that they were at the German position on the bridge over the River Orne. I was challenged again as I re-joined my comrades.

At the time of the airborne attack on the canal bridge the German defenders ran off without firing a shot. D Company occupied their position, keeping a look-out for a counter-attack.

Thus, A, B & C Companies, along with Battalion HQ continued south with the Caen Canal to their left towards Blainville in the early evening with supporting elements of the 13th/18th Hussars from 27th Armoured Brigade. A delaying force of *192.*

Panzergrenadier was encountered outside Blainville, with heavy machine-gun and 88mm fire slowing progress considerably. Two Shermans were immediately hit and brewed up, with the turret of one being blown clear of its hull. A number of casualties were suffered included one of the forward observation officers, however a B Company platoon under Lieutenant D. A. Field was ordered to make an assault on houses ahead of them. In this they were successful, taking no losses and capturing a small number of prisoners.

Captain Harry Illing
Officer Commanding A Company, 2nd Battalion Royal Warwickshire Regiment

> Evening was almost upon us as we pushed forward from the burning village.... Almost immediately two tanks were hit, one of them the artillery observer's.... It was now quite dark, and we reconnoitred forward to select our position. As the recce party moved down a side track one member flung himself to the ground and opened fire; we followed suit. Luckily our blow got home first. A German recce party evidently on the same job as ourselves had come off second best. We dug in and settled down for the night.... The night was warm, and guns kept firing. During the night our only interruptions were the Germans who strayed into our positions neatly to be put in the bag.

Just after midnight, the exhausted men of the battalion made camp for the night on the outskirts of Blainville to the sound of Royal Artillery gunfire. At this point, the close of D-Day, 6 June 1944, the Battalion War Diary records they had suffered 4 killed and 35 wounded, however in the Commonwealth War Graves Cemetery in Normandy, there are seven members of the battalion listed as having been killed on 6 June 1944. It is difficult to say which is correct, the likelihood is that the War Diary is correct, and that three of the seven headstones should probably say 7 June – see below. Private James Arch, wounded on 6 June, would later die of his wounds received while in hospital in Brighton on 2 August 1944, and is buried at London Road Cemetery in Coventry.

Lieutenant Kingston St John Adams
A Company, 2nd Battalion Royal Warwickshire Regiment

> Around 1 a.m. the company reached a road junction and orders were given to halt for the night. My platoon took up its positions in a large wood with good fields of fire and view along 'rides' through the wood. We hastily dug in and arranged for as many as possible to get some well-earned sleep, putting sentries out where necessary, my platoon Sgt [Day] and I took it in turns to remain on duty. At around 3 a.m. the company commander visited and seemed quite satisfied. We had two scares during the night.
>
> The first was a burst of machine-gun fire at the far end of one of the 'rides' in the woods. I sent three men to investigate but they returned with nothing to report
>
> The second 'incident' was the appearance of a big, fat German soldier strolling through the wood apparently completely unaware of our presence! He was removed to Company HQ for questioning and probably remained a PoW for the

rest of the war! Fearing his arrival might have been a trap to locate our positions I stood the platoon 'to', expecting an enemy fighting patrol to attack us, but nothing happened.

Captain Alastair J. M. Bannerman
Officer Commanding Anti-Tank Platoon, 2nd Battalion Royal Warwickshire Regiment

The CO ordered a stop and we dug ourselves in by the streets of Benouville. A cold night, I put out my guns, and then Toon-Poynton and I tried to warm each other by huddling together under his gas cape in a ditch, but without success. Only a terrible cramp in the bottom!

***Major* Hans von Luck**
Panzergrenadierregiment Nr 125, 21. Panzerdivision

So the tragedy took its course. After only a few hours, the brave fighting units in the coastal fortifications could no longer withstand the enemy pressure, or else they were smashed by the Allied naval guns; while a Panzer Division, ready to engage, lay motionless behind the front and powerful Allied bomber formations, thanks to complete air superiority, covered the coastal divisions and Caen with concentrated attacks. In the early hours of the morning, from the hills east of Caen, we saw the gigantic Allied armada, the fields littered with transport gliders and the numerous observation balloons over the landing fleet, with the help of which the heavy naval guns subjected us to precision fire.[17]

Captain Harry Illing
A Company, 2nd Battalion Royal Warwickshire Regiment

Some Huns came in and surrendered during that short night. A brief rest and on again at half-past four. Carefully we probed into the next village and through it, but the Boche had gone. Into the houses and defence prepared – then breakfast – including biscuits and bully and some fresh milk from the French. So far so good.... We had scuppered some Boche, were in good spirits and confident.

With the capture of Caen, the end goal for the 185th Infantry Brigade on D-Day, the 2nd Warwicks were still short. 2nd KSLI and 1st Norfolks had twice become bogged down and despite their route having been subject to intense RAF bombing and naval bombardment in the build-up, they were faced with a determined and well dug in enemy, able to constantly rain mortar and machine-gun fire on the advancing troops. The delays at Hillman prevented further advances and congestion on the beach prevented adequate armoured support being available for the attempted assaults. Eventually the invading forces prevailed, passing down the main road to Caen and capturing Beuville without resistance. They then faced a strong defence at Biéville, the next village they

17 These were not, of course, observation balloons but the anti-aircraft barrage balloons which protected the ships of the invasion force.

encountered, as the effects of the *Panzerregiment Nr 21* advance towards the coast was felt. After fierce fighting at Biéville, the 2nd KSLI rested just south of the village to consolidate before its next focus. As Y Company of the 2nd KSLI advanced towards the outskirts of Lebisey, machine-gun fire soon held them firm amid the realisation that the village of Lebisey boasted a strong defensive force, at this point the decision was made that it was beyond the ability of the strung out infantry battalion to continue the push to Caen via Lebisey, with the 1st Norfolks and 2nd KSLI still 4km short, the advance on Caen ended. Casualties in the 185th Infantry Brigade on D-Day totalled 232 dead, wounded and missing.

Men from a Battalion of the Royal Warwickshire Regiment who took part in the exercise, showed a great interest in the tanks when they were conducted round the marshalling area by officers and men of the Royal Tank Regiment. (Photo: © IWM H32695)

Pre-Invasion photograph of the 2nd Battalion Officers (Left to Right) Back Row: 5th Captain Bannerman, 6th Lieutenant Adams. Second Row: 4th Lieutenant Healey. Front Row: 2nd Major Brock, 3rd Captain Pike, 5th Lieutenant Colonel Herdon, 6th Captain Batt, 7th Captain Allan, 8th Major Bundock. (Photo: Royal Regiment of Fusiliers Museum Warwick)

Remember :—

"THE Lord is my light and my salvation : whom shall I fear? The Lord is the strength of my life : of whom shall I be afraid."—*Ps. 27, 1.*

In heavenly love abiding,
  No change my heart shall fear ;
And safe is such confiding,
  For nothing changes here :
The storm may roar without me,
  My heart may low be laid,
But God is round about me,
  And can I be dismayed ?

JESUS said: "Lo, I am with you alway, even unto the end of the world."—*Matt. 28, 20.*

A Daily Prayer.

ALMIGHTY God, to whom all hearts are open, help me to face whatever comes with complete trust in Thee. If I forget Thee, do not Thou forget me. Give me strength and courage to fulfil my duty, and prosper our cause until victory is won. Defend from all evil my loved ones at home, and help them to keep the home-fires brightly burning. Help us to preserve our mutual loyalties that, whatever happens, nothing may dismay our courage, spoil our faith, or ruin our characters: through Jesus Christ our Lord.

HOLY Father in Thy mercy,
  Hear our anxious prayer ;
Keep our loved ones, now far distant,
  'Neath Thy care.

2002.49.6

The Royal Warwickshire Regiment.

With the Padre's Good Wishes.

"BE STRONG AND OF A GOOD COURAGE ; BE NOT AFRAID, NEITHER BE THOU DISMAYED ; FOR THE LORD THY GOD IS WITH THEE WHITHERSOEVER THOU GOEST."—*Joshua 1, 9.*

Prayer card issued to members of the regiment before the invasion. (Photo: Royal Regiment of Fusiliers Museum Warwick)

Men of the Warwickshire Regiment digging-in alongside a country lane outside Beuville, north of Caen. 17 June 1944. (Photo: © IWM B5765)

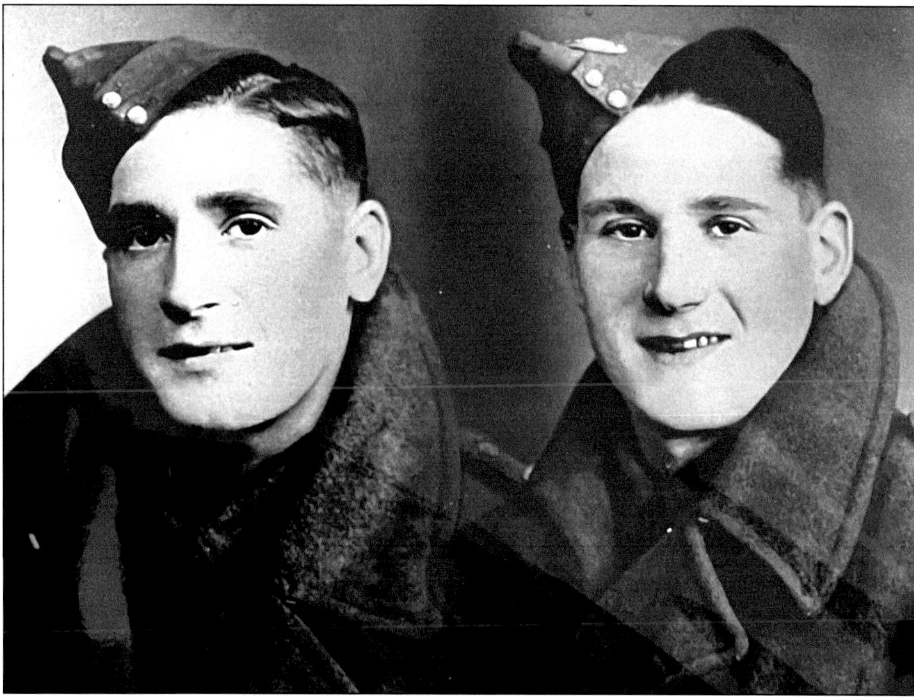

Corporal Charlie Tweed and his brother, Sapper Bill Tweed, Royal Engineers. (Photo: Ernie Tweed)

Corporal Charlie Tweed, C Company, 2nd Battalion, the Royal Warwickshire Regiment. Authors Great Uncle. (Photo: Ernie Tweed)

William Tweed, father of Charlie and Bill; served with the Royal Warwickshire Regiment in The Great War. (Photo: Ernie Tweed)

Company Sergeant Major F. Launchbury of Reading. Before the outbreak of the war he had served in Palestine, Egypt & India with the 1st Battalion, The Royal Warwickshire Regiment. He transferred to the 2nd Battalion before the Normandy invasion. (Photo: © IWM B5830)

Sergeant William Joseph Gray of the Mortar Platoon, 2nd Battalion, Royal Warwickshire Regiment, at the wheel of a Bren Carrier. 20 June 1944. Sergeant Gray died on 22 November 1944 during the fighting in The Netherlands. © IWM (B 5831)

Private F. Price and Lance Sergeant F. Quelch of 2nd Battalion, Royal Warwickshire Regiment loading a 6-pdr anti-tank gun at Beuville, north of Caen, 20 June 1944. Both men had served as pre-war regulars in the 1st Battalion under the then Lieutenant Colonel Bernard Law Montogomery. (Photo: © IWM B5836)

Company Sergeant Major Mills, D Company, 2nd Battalion, Royal Warwickshire Regiment, writing home from his dugout somewhere in Normandy. 2 July 1944. Company Sergeant Major Mills was wounded during Operation Goodwood. (Photo: © IWM B 6306)

Above left: Captain Alastair Bannerman. OC AT Platoon, 2nd Battalion, Royal Warwickshire Regiment. (Photo: Bannerman Family)

Above right: Captain Harry Illing. OC A Coy, 2nd Battalion, Royal Warwickshire Regiment. (Photo: Illing Family)

Right: Captain Peter Batt, Adjutant, 2nd Battalion Royal Warwickshire Regiment. (Photo: Clare Linsell)

Jean and Peter Batt's wedding, April 1944. Lieutenant Philip Healy is best man. (Photo: Clare Linsell)

Privates Steve 'Topper' Brown, Fred Forknall and Wilf Sommerville then of 70th Battalion, Royal Warwickshire Regiment in 1941. Fred would later transfer to the Ox & Bucks with Steve and Wilf transferring to 2nd Battalion the Royal Warwickshire Regiment. (Photo: Rob Pettitt)

Pre-Invasion photo of five members of the 2nd Battalion Royal Warwickshire Regiment. Front row left: Private John Gundy, front row right: Private Albert Buckley. (Photo: Lindsay Brookes)

Painting of the 2nd Warwicks landing on D-Day by Gilbert Soloman. Now housed in the Officers Mess of the Royal Regiment of Fusiliers, Tidworth Barracks. (Painting in the Collection of the Regiment. Author's photograph)

Corporal Ronald Owen Nicholls, 2nd Battalion, Royal Warwickshire Regiment. Private Owen was killed on 7 June 1944, aged 33. (Photo: Jason Woods and Royal Warwickshire Regiment Re-enactment Facebook Group)

Captain Walter Pike, 2nd Battalion, Royal Warwickshire Regiment was captured on 7 June 1944. (Photo: Jason Woods and Royal Warwickshire Regiment Re-enactment Facebook Group)

Temporary grave of Lieutenant Colonel Herdon, killed in action on 7 June 1944 in the battle for Lebisey Wood. (Photo: Royal Regiment of Fusiliers Museum Warwick)

Sergeant R. Jennings, 2nd Battalion, Royal Warwickshire Regiment, was awarded the Military Medal for patrol work around Lebisey Wood on the evening of 6 June 1944 prior to the attack on the following day. (Photo: Will Thatcher)

Private George Albert Brueton, 2nd Battalion, Royal Warwickshire Regiment, killed 25 June 1944, Aged 33. (Photo: Jason Woods)

5

Lebisey Wood

In the very early hours of 7 June, in anticipation of a counter-attack, the beleaguered 2nd KSLI was withdrawn. As the 2nd Warwicks woke early, they were first tasked with clearing the final defenders from Blainville, pushing *192. Panzergrenadier* south towards Hérouville. While D Company remained defending the bridges at Bénouville, the remainder of the battalion took up positions south of Blainville in preparation for their next attack – Lebisey Wood.

Captain Harry Illing
A Company, 2nd Battalion Royal Warwickshire Regiment

Orders for this attack were given in the dark off the map and at that stage no visual reconnaissance of the objective or the approaches to it could be done.

The mopping up of Blainville in the early morning of 7 June (my birthday) was quickly accomplished and the stage set for the 'Battle of Lebisey'. The plan contained a major fundamental flaw, an elementary error; the start line was not secured. Indeed, it was nearly halfway towards the edge of the objective from Blainville.

***Leutnant* Hans Hoeller**
8. Kompanie, 2. Bataillon, Panzergenadierregiment Nr 192

In the morning of 7 June, there still was no absolutely clear situation report on anyone's desk. All we knew was that the British had already bypassed us west of Benouville, standing in Biéville and, presumably, Blainville. I realised that from now on we would go on nothing but fire runs. There was no overarching coordination of our division's units to be expected; instead, we would attempt to extinguish one fire after the other in our immediate surroundings. Until we ran out of water…

Captain Harry Illing
A Company, 2nd Battalion Royal Warwickshire Regiment

I climbed up a water tower at one end of Blainville to see if I could…. see the objective which was the woods at the top of Lebisey Hill and the start line which was a stream which was in fact a very formidable anti-tank obstacle, a very deep and wide ditch, a natural anti-tank obstacle.

The village of Lebisey was the last point in the advance to Caen some 3km away. The village sat atop a rise, thick woodland lay to the east on a slope some 3,000m south-west of the battalion's position south of Blainville. At 0730 hours orders were issued by Lieutenant Colonel Herdon that A, B and C Companies were to attack at 0845 hours, with A & B Companies tasked with directly attacking the eastern part of the wood (A on the left and B on the right) and C Company was: 'To follow up, pass through and clear the western half.'[1] D Company was to join up with the rest of the battalion once relieved at the bridges. The attack would be preceded by a considerable barrage from both brigade artillery and a naval cruiser just offshore. However, as the leading companies made for the start line at 0800 hours, things began to unravel. The battalion's carriers and anti-tank guns were deemed unable to reach the rifle companies due to boggy ground near B & C Companies' forming up point and had become bogged down in swampy ground, and A Company had been held up by snipers.

B & C Companies had made it to the start line along the Le Dan stream to the north of the wood, despite the attention of enemy snipers. The Le Dan formed a natural anti-tank barrier and prevented armoured support moving up. Without the expected forces to hand, no carriers and no anti-tank support, Lieutenant Colonel Herdon made the decision to delay the attack until 0945 hours, cancelling the artillery programme. Unfortunately, communications with B & C Companies failed at this crucial moment and they began their advance across the cornfields precisely on time at 0845 hours as per their last received orders, Herdon was unable to send a runner to hold them firm as movement to these battalions was impeded by enemy mortar fire. The only artillery support available was from the 3-inch anti-tank guns of two M10 'Wolverines' from 20th Anti-Tank Regiment RA, which had managed to negotiate the Le Dan anti-tank ditch and were able to fire high explosive and smoke rounds onto the objective.

***Leutnant* Hans Hoeller**
8. Kompanie, 2. Bataillon, Panzergenadierregiment Nr 192

> I had posted two of my men up on the ridge as forward observers. They reported that right ahead of us, on the southern outskirts of Blainville, the first British had shown themselves. As soon as the opportunity arose, I reconnoitred the surroundings with my two runners. After sighting the terrain, we found a good location. Between the road over the ridge, along the Caen Canal, there was a narrow stretch of woodland.
>
> Our own II Battalion now was in a defensive position northeast of Caen stretching from Hérouville to the Orne bank near Colombelles…
>
> There was noticeable activity left on the ridge ahead of Lebisey as well as to our right around Colombelles…

1 TNA WO 171/1387, '2nd Battalion, The Royal Warwickshire Regiment, War Diary,' 7 June 1944.

Captain Harry Illing
Officer Commanding A Company, 2nd Battalion Royal Warwickshire Regiment

> I went forward to recce in my carrier and had to run the gauntlet, but the carrier got us through. The company, moving up to the assembly area under CSM Francis, hit trouble from two machine guns and snipers and were shaken up, suffering about 10 casualties. The attack was put back, but at last B and C went into the attack. I was to pass through and clear up the rear enemy locality.

At this time, it was believed that the woods were not strongly defended, unbeknownst to the CO the two companies were advancing unsupported, wading steadily through the waist deep corn, towards the forward sections of *4. Kompanie, Panzergrenadierregiment Nr 125* and around 40 Panzer IVs of *Panzerregiment Nr 22* of *Panzerdivision Nr 21*, who had moved into position unnoticed during the night.[2] *21. Panzer* knew the ground well, having trained in the area recently, giving them at additional advantage as they dug in, making use of pre-sited defences for this very eventuality. Evidently, they had received little damage from the attentions of the two Wolverines.

Captain Walter Pike
Adjutant, 2nd Battalion Royal Warwickshire Regiment

> What our intelligence didn't know was that, quite coincidentally, the German 21st Panzer Division was conducting exercises in the area, so we met unexpected resistance.... Fortunately, the British airborne troops were successful in their operation to protect the eastern flank of the attack... Our men attacked but were knocked about very badly...

Corporal Alec Graham Pugh
Carrier Platoon, 2nd Battalion, Royal Warwickshire Regiment

> They then had to advance on Lebisey Wood .... which was up a huge slope.... a huge cornfield. If one had gone through Lebisey Wood for about a mile, you could have then looked down into Caen.... We had been informed that this wood and area were held by inferior German troops belonging to the *Todt* Organisation and air force personnel and that the nearest.... panzer regiment was 50 miles away.... and that no way would they be able to move that far to threaten, but they had, they were in the wood, their panzer grenadiers and their tanks and stuff had already taken up position.

Private Ted Bedford
D Company, 2nd Battalion Royal Warwickshire Regiment

> Shortly after daybreak on 7 June two German bombers, Junkers 88s, were spotted following the line of the river and heading towards us. Before we had time to react three Spitfires appeared at the rear of the two bombers and shot them down. Both

2 Hans Hoeller (Andreas Hartinger, ed.), *D-Day Tank Hunter*, ([Germany], Privately Published, 2022).

crashed into the riverbank about 100 yards in front of us. All was quiet for the next few hours and we were then informed that sufficient airborne troops had arrived to relieve us. D Company was then ordered to re-join the rest of the 2nd Battalion for the attack on Lebisey.

On the way we passed a British Sherman tank with its turret lying on the ground with the top half of a body in it and another scorched body, completely naked, lying beside the tank. Perhaps the rigorous training encouraging us to push on helped us to cope with such sights and ignore them.

Sergeant Bob Barnett (Intelligence Sergeant)
B Company, 2nd Battalion Royal Warwickshire Regiment

The CO committed all of us, up we went. And we really were full of confidence, we thought it was going to be pretty easy. We went over an anti-tank ditch, and I left a lot of my heavy gear there intending to fetch it when we'd taken the hill we were so confident. Then we got further and everything opened up, machine-gun fire and all kinds, mortar, artillery, everything.

Now with A Company in position, Herdon moved them and Battalion HQ forward to support the leading companies, while also instructing Bannerman's anti-tank platoon and the battalion carriers to sweep round to the west, through 1st Norfolks and hold position south of Biéville until ordered forward to consolidate. The German troops held their fire until the leading sections of 2nd Warwicks were around 200m distant. Cornfields offer very little cover from small arms and machine-gun fire and casualties were taken immediately, but those still standing made a break and advanced on the woods, where they dug in and sited themselves well.

Lieutenant Dockerty, B Company, bravely led his platoon in a charge against a group of defenders, however, in the face of heavy fire none reached their objective and all became casualties, with Lieutenant Dockerty killed just a few metres short of the enemy line. Alan Dockerty attended Jesus College, Oxford and was awarded a Blue for Football in 1941. Amidst a hail of bullets and explosions both A & B Companies were pinned down and unable to move due to the heavy fire. The lack of support was starting to tell, and the thick woodland the men had hoped to find refuge in only made matters worse, as explosions rent the trees apart adding lethal splinters of trunk and branch to the shrapnel of the shells. Lieutenant A. G. Wilson, OC of the Assault Pioneer Platoon was killed during the attack, Captain Illing and Lieutenant Adams were both wounded.

Captain Harry Illing
Officer Commanding A Company, 2nd Battalion Royal Warwickshire Regiment

We formed up on a very convex slope, so that we were out of sight of the top of Lebisey Hill and in the fields in front was higher standing corn. So I gave out my orders, this was where the thing started to go wrong. Unfortunately, the two companies on my right had got out of touch and the attack was postponed for one hour, that order did not teach the two companies on my right and our support weapons, particularly the armoured carriers, couldn't get across the natural obstacle of the stream and ditch and so had to be sent round to the road that was running parallel to the one we had advanced along. So the two companies on my right started off and the CO realising this, I was ordered to go off too, so we started off onto our attack unfortunately without the fire support that we should have received, so off we went climbing up through the high corn, out of view of the enemy up the convex slope towards the top, no problems and indeed no problems until we got to the beginning of the wooded area. We were met with very substantial fire, really a wall of fire, if I can describe it as such without being dramatic, was more than could possibly be penetrated by us.

Lieutenant Kingston St John Adams
A Company, 2nd Battalion Royal Warwickshire Regiment

We did our best to get into the wood – two sections of my platoon moved up, covered by the other two – leapfrogging. I did not have a sense of the casualties we were taking, but I think I lost three or four men approaching the wood. You could hear shouts and screams but you couldn't do much about it. They were spraying heavy machine-gun fire at us. They couldn't see us clearly. I had been told to get into the wood and that is what I tried to do. The enemy fire seemed to get stronger as we got closer.

Sergeant John Hawkes
2nd Battalion, the Royal Warwickshire Regiment

Now, they went through this field up to this Lebisey Wood, which strikes horror into the thoughts of anyone who was in the Warwicks at that time. The Germans saw them coming, they thought well, this isn't a very bright move on their part, but they let them get to within a hundred yards of the wood, then they opened up with everything they'd got. And A and B Companies, were more or less wiped out.

Captain Harry Illing
A Company, 2nd Battalion Royal Warwickshire Regiment

My forward platoons came under withering fire from very close range.... My men, with very great discipline, went forward through intense fire. They responded magnificently. I was shot and about 20 minutes later shot again. The Hun were cunningly concealed. The Germans stuck to their guns, and by God they had a hell of a lot of automatics. I lay in the middle of the field – only about 50 yards from the Boche; my men tried to get in with the bayonet, but few got to the next hedgerow. I managed to crawl flat on my back to the little ditch. I was very weak and had lost a lot of blood. I was able to get information from my platoons. They had all suffered. Tiny Adams was wounded. Charles Jarvis was missing.... John Erskine was OK but had had his boot laces cut by a bullet.

As D Company continued their delayed move, having been relieved of their defensive duties in Bénouville, unfortunately amidst the fog of war, not everything is as it seems.

Private Ted Bedford
D Company, 2nd Battalion Royal Warwickshire Regiment

At the edge of Blainville we followed a path which led us to the base of a ridge where we saw what we thought were German troops. We fired from the hip as we approached.... but as we got closer we realised they were British survivors from A Company's main attack on Lebisey. I was not aware of causing any causalities in the confusion and I hope that this was really the case.

We followed orders to carry on up the ridge. When we reached the top we looked down on to a German tank with its crew and about a dozen British prisoners. We wanted to fire at the enemy but refrained because we might have hit our own people.

Major T. L. Brock
HQ Company, 2nd Battalion Royal Warwickshire Regiment

D Company [Major T. G. Bundock], having been relieved on the bridge then arrived. Unfortunately, owing to lack of information, they mistook Battalion Headquarters for Germans and put in an attack which luckily did very little damage.

Major Mike Ryan
Officer Commanding Support Company, 2nd Battalion Royal Warwickshire Regiment

Due to the breakdown in wireless communications we had little or no artillery or tank support. Infantry wireless sets in those days were cumbersome, heavy, and prone to break down.

Our leading companies got within 200 yards of the enemy position but suffered heavily. We could not get over the crest without being mown down.

We were out of touch with our Brigade HQ but managed to maintain contact through our gunner forward observation officer's set which was more powerful than ours.

We were literally pinned down above the Lebisey feature. We dug in a bit. The enemy could not come forward. To make matters worse ATK guns, Bren carriers and mortars were under Brigade control at Benouville[3] awaiting our capture of the Lebisey feature.

Lieutenant Kingston St John Adams
A Company 2nd Battalion Royal Warwickshire Regiment

We took cover behind a small bank which ran round the side of the wood. Here I halted temporarily to arrange for smoke and fire from the rear section to cover our further move forward. But with enemy fire getting heavier and being unable to locate its exact position because of the thickness of the wood, we were unable to make much progress forward, so I tried to move round to the right flank of the wood, hoping to find an opening less strongly defended. Control at this stage was

3 Whilst Maj. Ryan states Benouville, it was in fact Bieville.

> getting more and more difficult to maintain, with many men becoming casualties and contact with Coy HQ temporarily lost. A small party of the platoon managed to enter a clearing in the wood and did make a bit of temporary progress, but soon met more enemy fire. At this stage I was hit by a phosphorous grenade which burst over my legs and I received a bullet in my left hand which together with the burning of my legs put me out of action although I was later casevaced to our own rear area and back to the UK.[4]

Moving forwards with his men, Lieutenant Colonel Herdon was struck in the head by machine-gun fire and, sadly, was killed. Herdon was a respected and well-loved CO, not least because of his ability to readily provide fresh packets of cigarettes to his men as he moved between positions.

Brigadier Kenneth Pearce-Smith OBE
Officer Commanding 185th Infantry Brigade

> Meanwhile the Warwicks had reached the Lebisey Woods and all hell was let loose – machine guns, Spandaus, etc. Poor 'Jumbo' Herdon was killed instantly, as were many of his troops; his second in command, Major Kreyer, gave the order to retire. Colonel Herdon was my youngest CO, an excellent soldier and a great loss. I was very distressed but General Rennie had kept on emphasising the need for speed. But believing that panzer troops might be at Lebisey in strength, I should have told him that this attack would be courting disaster.

Sergeant Bob Barnett (Intelligence Sergeant)
B Company, 2nd Battalion Royal Warwickshire Regiment

> I was with the second in command.... Robin Kreyer... spotted that the CO had been killed and so it was essential to get across to him. He just strode across between the bursts of machine-gun fire and I went across with him.... And there the CO was, he was riddled, and Robin said, you better see if the CO's got any ammunition, so I looked in his pouches and there was no ammunition, they were full of 20 packets of players, but it was a real shaker that he was dead because he was a very good CO and we liked him too.

Captain Harry Illing
Officer Commanding A Company, 2nd Battalion Royal Warwickshire Regiment

> I managed to get to Major Kreyer, who was going along the hedgerow – 100 yards from the Boche – with Battalion HQ. The Colonel lay shot through the mouth. We hit back, but ammunition was low.

4 Casevaced is military slang for casualty evacuation.

Captain Alastair J. M. Bannerman
Officer Commanding Anti-Tank Platoon, 2nd Battalion Royal Warwickshire Regiment

> Tall, elegant and gallant, he was a charming and gifted leader whom I would have followed anywhere. It wasn't his fault that we had no support, or that the wood was held by 21st Panzer Division, Rommel's old crack troops who knew all the tricks of the trade…

Captain Harry Illing
A Company, 2nd Battalion Royal Warwickshire Regiment

> Losing the Colonel was a great blow. He was shot right up front. He was a great friend to us all, and a very generous and fine leader. I never hope to have a better commanding officer, and very humbly I say it, a better friend.

Second in command, Major R. G. Kreyer took temporary command of the battalion. With the anti-tank platoon in reserve the situation might have been different until fate once against intervened. Frustrated at just listening to a battle, Captain Bannerman edged his platoon forward passed Battalion HQ meeting a platoon of 2nd Norfolks, who to his dismay were starting to withdraw. Alas, due to either poor communications or a simple misunderstanding, Brigadier Smith incorrectly believed that Lebisey Woods had been taken and now was time to consolidate.[5]

Captain Alastair J. M. Bannerman
Officer Commanding Anti-Tank Platoon, 2nd Battalion Royal Warwickshire Regiment

> Suddenly the brigadier dashed up in a flap…. with his red tabs blazing. He told me the battalion had captured the hill and I was to proceed on down the road and join them as there were Jerry tanks about…. so I saluted and called my chaps, already briefed, and told them to follow me…

Sergeant John Hawkes
2nd Battalion, the Royal Warwickshire Regiment

> In the meantime, due to all this lack of communication the carriers in Bieville, had been ordered up onto the ridge, by a brigadier who said the ridge was clear. Which it definitely wasn't.

A long procession of assorted vehicles set forth; motorcycles, halftracks, carriers and trucks. One halftrack, driven by Lance Bombardier Hyde RA, carried Captain J. Lee, the Royal Artillery Forward Officer Bombardment attached to 2nd Warwicks. Captain Lee had had an active morning and didn't shy away from action, he was seen by one witness during the morning firing a Bren Gun from the rear of his vehicle to suppress an enemy attack, while he was searching for a new observation post. As the different platoons of the Support Company moved forward they came under increasingly heavy fire.

5 Bannerman, *If I Don't Come Home, Letters from D-Day*, p.60.

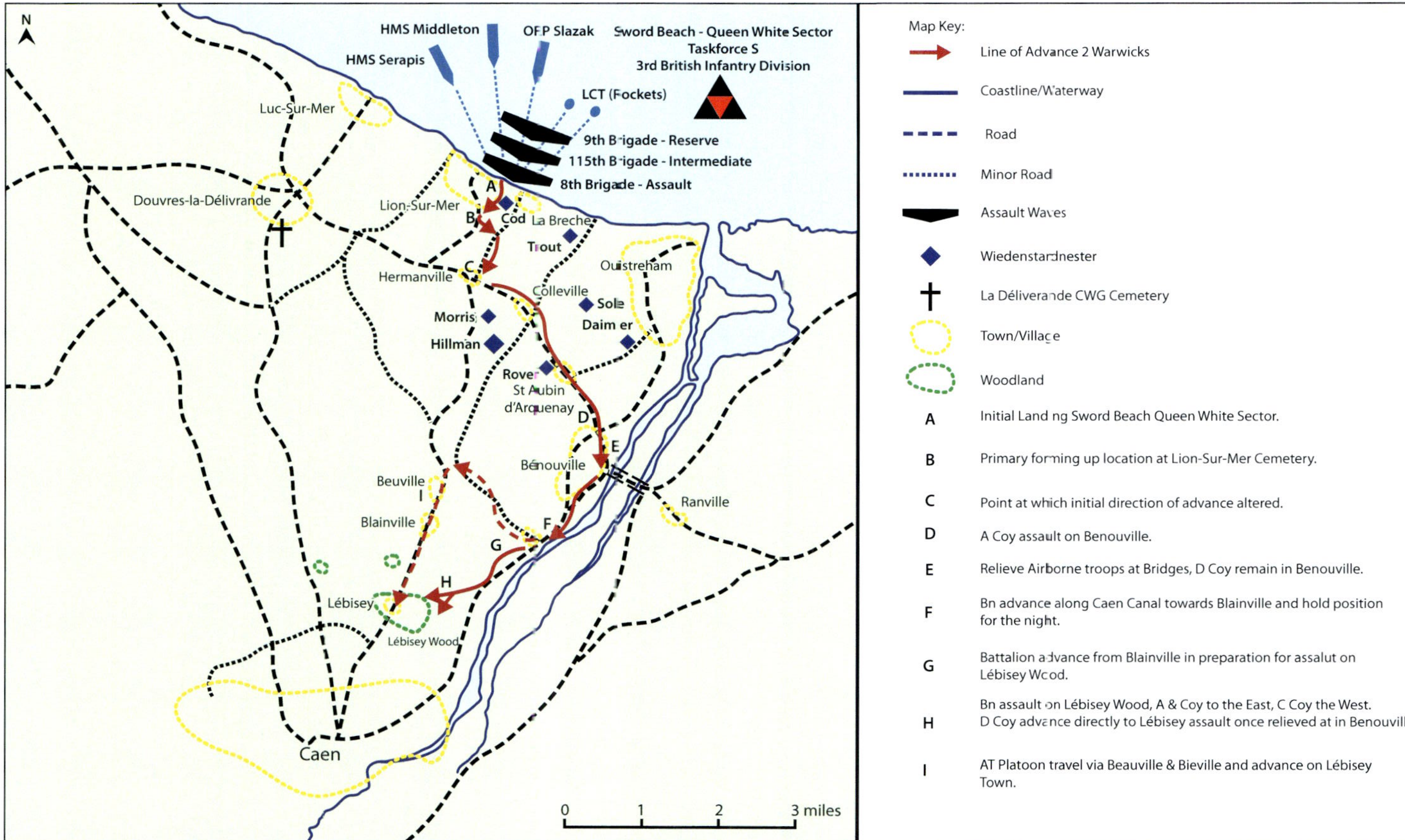

The Sword Area landing and lodgement zone, and the approximate route taken by the 2nd Battalion Royal Warwickshire Regiment on 6 and 7 June 1944.

Captain Walter Pike
Adjutant, 2nd Battalion Royal Warwickshire Regiment

> I was ordered to take all the vehicles via a different route and try to join up with my battalion in the wood, which I was (mistakenly) told they had captured. We were the nearest Allied troops to the city of Caen but had no tanks, only ordinary vehicles. Mine was the fourth vehicle in the line and suddenly – boom – the first truck disappeared, then the second, then the third: there was a German tank just picking us off one by one.

After negotiating around Walter Pike's burning halftrack, Captain Lee's halftrack was most likely knocked out by a teller anti-tank mine, with him and the crew suffering terrible leg wounds. Captain Lee's wife, Olive, received a telegram notifying her that her husband had been reported MIA and she waited for many weeks in the hope of news that he was a PoW, until 31 August 1944, when she received a letter from a G. P. Rogers of 223 Field Ambulance, RAMC to inform her that her husband had tragically died of his wounds peacefully in his care in the early evening of 7 June.[6]

The anti-tank platoon headed down the narrow road in their six carriers but after about 800m 'all hell let loose.'[7] Incoming rounds whizzing over their heads, the platoon had cover from the high banks along the road, so were able to continue. Still under heavy fire they couldn't stop, so Bannerman decided that speed was of the essence and urged them forward and the carriers accelerated firing wildly to each side with their Sten and Bren Guns. As they approached the now wrecked village of Lebisey, they could see German troops running between the ruined houses as they sped on into the middle of the enemy formation. Only Bannerman's carrier made it this far, the other five had been knocked out either by mines or by machine-gun fire, only to see the bewildered faces of a Panzer IV crew, who were apparently so surprised, as they watched this lone British carrier whizzing down the rubble strewn road, that they didn't open fire, they soon recovered their wits however.

Captain Alastair J. M. Bannerman
Officer Commanding Anti-Tank Platoon, 2nd Battalion Royal Warwickshire Regiment

> We couldn't stop to say hello and tore on. At last we were out of the village and on the.... main road to Caen. I felt we couldn't go on any further and attack Caen alone with one gun! So we stopped and bailed out in a wild frenzy and I gave the one order I had always felt certain of never giving: "Action Rear." .... Our gun drill wasn't bad, though I think the language was far from drill book. The gun was soon firing, and how, we hit and holed the tank which had poked out from a house after we had cascaded past .... I remember the loader.... quite imperturbable, and another Birmingham lad firing the gun with a gleaming smile and a flood of obscenity.

6 Lee, Adrian, *Death of my 2nd Warwick Father*, (Unpublished, 2004).
7 Bannerman, *If I Don't Come Home, Letters from D-Day*, p.60.

After letting off eight rounds, the rate of incoming fire increased and suddenly the carrier went up in flames, hit by a high explosive round setting off all the unused ammunition and putting the gun out of action. With a cry of: 'Everyone for himself, good luck,'[8] the Captain and his team ran into a field in an attempt to hide in the wheat, but lying there with only a single grenade which he had already pulled the pin from, Bannerman realised that the tracks of trampled wheat would lead the enemy straight to him.

Captain Alastair J. M. Bannerman
Officer Commanding Anti-Tank Platoon, 2nd Battalion Royal Warwickshire Regiment

I peered up over the wheat and to my despair and horror saw a German pointing a *Schmeisser* at me and shouting and jerking his gun to tell me to get up. I saw behind him three of my chaps with their hands up and a tracked vehicle covering us all.... so I stood up with the grenade in my right hand and my arms above my head.... I pointed to it with my left hand and said "grenade" rather feebly. The German bellowed again so I chucked it hard over my shoulder behind me and it went off a few yards away in the wheat. I was then marched off with my men. Why I didn't get shot outright I shall never know.

Sergeant John Hawkes
2nd Battalion, the Royal Warwickshire Regiment

The scenario was we had 18 carriers, six Bren Guns, six mortars and six anti-tank guns proceed up a very narrow lane, like a Devon country lane with banks up either side and the Germans couldn't believe their eyes. They said well don't do anything, just let them come! And they went over the ridge and the crossroad and then the Germans gave them everything they had. And every member of those 18 carriers with all the support weapons was either killed or taken prisoner.

Sergeant Bob Barnett (Intelligence Sergeant)
B Company 2nd Battalion Royal Warwickshire Regiment

I had to carry the key to the code for the day and various other things to do with the intelligence job and so I thought I'd better bury these, we were surrounded by now and well forward of the main line, I thought we were all going to be taken prisoner.... there was intermittent fire, and every time you wriggled there seemed to be a shot, one shot opened up my first finger and I tried to bandage it up with my field dressing but that was hopeless.... Peter Lamb the intelligence officer had got hold of a Bren Gun and he said to me will you be my number two? So I was crawling about with Peter, dragging this Bren Gun around.... and then when it went dark, we managed to get back down the hill and we sorted ourselves out in the field behind the King's Shropshire Light infantry who were forming a firm base behind us.... We were in some disarray, we'd lost a lot of men and a lot of equipment.

8 Bannerman, *If I Don't Come Home, Letters from D-Day*, p.61.

Captain Harry Illing
Officer Commanding A Company, 2nd Battalion Royal Warwickshire Regiment

> Eventually, I was told to go back, and helped by Pte Nash, my Company Clerk, I managed to totter back. The wounded who could move wearily wended their way down the hill. At the bottom we tried to get the wounded back. I was able to help get them back away, and with the MO and was able to get some organisation going out of the confusion. Tom Bundock, who had been away with his Company, then came up.

Able to glimpse Caen in the distance through the trees, the battalion was agonisingly close. The three forward rifle companies, trapped under continuous fire were unable to move, forwards or backwards. At around 1500 hours, D Company, having left Bénouville, arrived and immediately attacked along the left flank, the north-eastern corner of the wood. Gallantly led by Major Tom Bundock,[9] brother-in-law of Lieutenant Colonel Herdon, D Company, with the inspiring actions of Sergeant Pittaway, relieved A Company after wiping out the German posts pinning them down. Both companies were able to continue their advance a short way until losing Lieutenant V. C. Walton, OC 17 platoon, D Company and being threatened by the Panzer IVs of *Panzerregiment Nr 22*, against which there was very little the infantry could do. The men worked their way deeper into the woods to avoid their attention. By 1600 hours the three companies were reported to be surrounded and by 1900 hours were almost out of ammunition.

Private Ted Bedford
D Company, 2nd Battalion Royal Warwickshire Regiment

> "Follow me!" ordered Major Bundock, our much-admired company commander. We followed him along the ditch until we reached the main road leading to Caen. We lined up beside the road and, together, made a dash to the other side.
>
> Our position was then at the rear of an orchard. We continued along a path intending to attack the enemy in the rear. The path, however, ended at a large area of open ground and it was unwise to proceed. We expected the Germans would anticipate an attack from that direction and we positioned ourselves at the rear of this orchard. We were fired on from the other side of the plantation and responded with rifle fire.
>
> Then we were fired on from four trees high on the ridge. We all responded. I put four shots into each tree and the fire was silenced. The enemy then began mortaring us
>
> Corporal Bowdidge, who was about five yards from me, called out: "I think I've been hit!" We were amazed that, although there were a number of lumps along his forearm, there was no blood.

9 As a captain, Tom Bundock had served as ADC to Montgomery earlier in the War.

Private Dennis Pettitt
D Company, 2nd Battalion Royal Warwickshire Regiment

> We were told to attack, we went into the wood, even in those days it wasn't a massive forest, it had little squares, more like copses, and then all of a sudden all around us were Tiger tanks,[10] bang bang bang bang, oh dear, we got orders to withdraw to the edge of the wood.... We'd lost a lot of officers and men, the CO went straight away, he was one of the first to get killed.... I remember seeing Lieutenant Dentith shot, I was with Nobby Moss and we both ran like fury to get back to the edge of the wood. We took off our assault jackets off so we could move and just had 100 rounds in bandolier form and hand grenades in your pockets. We then were under attack from their infantry, there was an anti-tank ditch.... about 20 yards in front of the wood and we all dived in there. And they mortared us and then two Messerschmitts came down and machine gunned us straight along the ditch, so we leaped out into the cornfields and then back again, up and down. In the end Tom Bundock said, "Right, we're moving to the other side of the lane," and he got the rest of the battalion together and we moved across the lane to the right hand side of that lane. And they mortared us again of course and that's where I got wounded...

Private Ted Bedford
D Company, 2nd Battalion Royal Warwickshire Regiment

> There was a shout that German tanks were coming and we should go back to the anti-tank ditch where we started the ascent. About 50 yards short of the ditch I threw myself into a hollow to sort myself out, expecting the enemy to follow behind me.
>
> A German machine gun fired at me every time I lifted my head. After several failed attempts to get out I settled into the hollow thinking that these were my last few minutes alive.
>
> I brought out a photo of my wife and a few boiled sweets. Later, I was aware of a shadow. It was a British artillery officer who asked what I was doing, "I've been pinned down by a machine gun, Sir," I replied.
>
> He said, "There's no firing now." So I grabbed the photograph and ran the 50 yards to the anti-tank ditch to join the others. The officer carried on to the top of the ridge and was immediately captured.

The 1st Norfolks had been sent forward in support, at first they had advanced in good order heading towards the wood. Now, in the face of heavy machine-gun and mortar fire, the reality hit both battalions that with the forces available to them that day Lebisey would not be captured, and the decision was made to withdraw. With the 1st Norfolks' stretcher-bearers helping bring back the wounded of 2nd Warwicks, they slipped away with 'what was left of the Warwicks' at 2230 hours.[11] One man, Corporal Ashdown,

10 Whilst the perception was they faced a Mark V1 Tiger Tank, they were in fact Panzer IV's.
11 John Lincoln, *Thank God and The Infantry* (Stroud: Sutton Publishing Limited, 1994), p.29.

wounded during the D Company attack, had been found by two German soldiers. Not knowing what to expect, he must have been relieved when they tended to his wounds and left him to crawl back to his own lines.

Captain Alastair J. M. Bannerman
Officer Commanding Anti-Tank Platoon, 2nd Battalion Royal Warwickshire Regiment

The noise increased again with the addition of small-arms fire and not so far away. I heard later it was the Norfolks's counter-attacking to help out my battalion which had been shot to pieces on the far edge of this large wood, and many even before they got into it.

Sergeant Major Russell King
C Company, 2nd Battalion Royal Warwickshire Regiment

We attacked this wood I remember, this Lebisey Wood, on the main line of attack, we suddenly found ourselves on the main Caen road.... The first initial assault that we were told we were going to make was B company and A company were going to assault this wood and we were going to follow through.... the opposition was that heavy, a lot of small arms stuff and snipers, that we got held up there...

Mostly snipers and B Company had had a run in on the top of this hill towards Lebisey village and I think they captured one or two Germans there. But it was all very fluid, I remember walking up the corn field and the corn seemed about chest height, and Captain Illing I remember of A Company.... Because they had gone ahead, and we were going through their company and Captain Illing was coming back and I remember he was wounded in his arm.... At the same time, we lost Jammy Wright, who was a sergeant.... just in front of us, he was wounded... he went down like a poleaxed steer, he was a massive fella.... and we found out he'd been shot clean through his ankle....

Captain Harry Illing
Officer Commanding A Company, 2nd Battalion Royal Warwickshire Regiment

Here we stuck. We were mortared again, but the expected Boche did not attack. I went back but could contact no one. Eventually, I sent back Lieutenant Taylor and received a message from the brigade major to withdraw. We were angry at being ordered back, but we had little ammunition and so I ordered a withdrawal. Back we marched some six miles, in good order. Here I met Captain Michael Hall, my 2iC, who with the other 2iCs had been left out of battle. I also saw Sammy Williams, our QM. I reported in person to brigade H.Q. and saw that all the information I had was taken down. Back to the battalion. Here were about 250 all ranks. First re-ammunition and then food. I was only just able to move then and so I was taken back to the FDS I knew it was goodbye to the lads. I was very moved when my men came up, tired as they were, to wish me luck.

Major Mike Ryan
Officer Commanding Support Company, 2nd Battalion Royal Warwickshire Regiment

We hung on in our positions just below the crest until about 1900 hrs when the 1st Royal Norfolks put in a diversionary attack on our left flank. Then we withdrew in an orderly manner.

I walked in front to keep the pace down. The soldiers responded well and came down in a dignified manner, in good order back to Bieville where we started to reorganise.

Private Dennis Pettitt
D Company, 2nd Battalion Royal Warwickshire Regiment

I was wounded and several were killed along that stretch in front of the woods, Tom Bundock came to me and took his jacket off, put it over me because I was shivering with shock and he jokingly said I promote you to a major. He said we've got to withdraw; we've got no tanks to hold off the Tigers.... there were several there, some very badly wounded, some killed, and that was when dusk came.... I was lying in the field, must have been only an hour or so and I'm lying there, Nobby Moss put a big field dressing around my shoulder and I'm lying there thinking Christ how to get out of this lot, I really thought I'd had it, we were fighting real hard nutcase Germans, and I heard a rustle in the hedgerow coming up from Bieville, and I heard this voice saying "Nifty, where are you?" and I thought oh my God. I said I'm here, he said. "It's Ginger Pike, with Big Robbo...." they were both in the boxing team with me.... they brought a stretcher, put me on the stretcher, we got down the lane towards Bieville and the Germans opened up on us. Fortunately, they opened up with 88mm shells, they dropped me in the middle of the road and.... these shells are going right over my head and right at the end of the lane there's a little curve and there was a Bren Gun carrier waiting for me, they strapped me on it, down to the central first aid with a proper medic and he said, "It's England for him."

Major Robin Kreyer
Second in Command, 2nd Battalion Royal Warwickshire Regiment

The Bn took the near edge of the wood but could not penetrate very far into it. We held the edge of the wood for the rest of the day under very heavy fire and were withdrawn at night. It was here that Col Herdon and Lt Wilson were killed and Illing wounded. Walton was wounded and is missing and Dockerty was wounded and I cannot find out whether he was evacuated or not. CSM Brown is also missing from this time. The Battalion behaved magnificently during the whole of the day and withdrew at night still in very good heart.

It's easy to think only of the fighting troops when we assess the different facets of a battle, but those men without a rifle in hand, were in just as much danger as anyone else. Particularly those of the RAMC, even though less than charitably known by some as 'Can't Manage a Rifle' or 'Rob All My Comrades', were doing their utmost to save the wounded.

Nursing Orderly First Class Jim Wisewell
223rd Field Ambulance Royal Army Medical Corps

> Although officially protected by the Geneva Convention which most of the Germans respected, a Field Ambulance was very much at the 'sharp end' of warfare and when evacuating casualties from the front line its personnel shared risks from shells and mortars, even if they were seldom the deliberate target of small-arms fire. So some of our men were KIA and some wounded and four were taken prisoners on D+1. Major Malcolm Oxley, Privates Rogers and Scoot, with Driver Cottrell took a stretcher-carrying jeep to Lebisey crossroads to try and bring out wounded from the 2 Warwicks who had caught a packet there. They ran straight into a German MG post and were captured. Driver Cottrell, being RASC and armed, was put into their PoW cage but the other three RAMC men were taken into Caen, questioned by the Gestapo without any effect, and sent to work in hospitals treating both German and British wounded.

Major Robin Kreyer
Second in Command, 2nd Battalion Royal Warwickshire Regiment

> Unfortunately, most of B Coy and Bn HQ Transport, trying to get up to join the rifle Coys were allowed to get right inside the German position and were then ambushed by Tanks and MGs. A large part of the crews of the vehicles escaped into the woods and cornfields and returned to the Bn during the night, having come back right through the German positions – a very fine effort. The Adjutant, Walter Pike, and Waterworth, Bannerman and Healey are all missing since this ambush, but all were seen by various people who got back and I feel that they are very probably all prisoners of war.

Now PoWs, Captains Bannerman, Pike (the adjutant) and Waterworth (OC Carrier Platoon) with Lieutenant Healey (OC Mortar Platoon) and the unfortunate other ranks from the Warwicks were marched into Lebisey itself with one corporal ominously muttering, "This is it Sir I'm afraid."[12] Around the same time as Major Bundock's D Company attack, Bannerman's adventures continued. As he was being driven away for interrogation, the car he was in crashed into a wall; taking his chance he made a run for it with his captor firing after him. Amidst the battle, he hid in the rubble as enemy tanks and troops passed close by. Later upon hearing what he took to be a British voice he raised his head, only to face, 'a black bearded scruffy German in a new type of black SS uniform with a particularly villainous face'[13] aiming an MP40 at him, most likely a member of incoming *12. SS Panzerdivision Hitlerjugend* if he was SS, although it was common for panzer soldiers, with their black uniform and deaths head collar badges

12 Bannerman, *If I Don't Come Home, Letters from D-Day,* p.61.
13 Bannerman, *If I Don't Come Home, Letters from D-Day,* p.63.

to be mistaken for SS. He was marched back past a number of British dead, with Bannerman recognising at least one fellow Warwicks officer amongst the fallen, to the rest of his men, with one calling out, "Didn't expect to see you again Sir!"[14] He was back in the bag.

Captain Walter Pike
Adjutant, 2nd Battalion Royal Warwickshire Regiment

Although my part in the main adventure was over within the first two days, we were proud to be taking part in the final attack on Germany – a triumphant return of the British Army to France after being forced to evacuate from Dunkirk in 1940.

Captain Alastair JM Bannerman
Officer Commanding Anti-Tank Platoon, 2nd Battalion Royal Warwickshire Regiment

It was getting dusky, and obviously we couldn't be left where we were. I then saw three fellow officers being brought in: the Adjutant Walter Pike, Carrier Officer Peter Waterworth and Mortar Officer Philip Healey. All looked white and shaken, and utterly despondent at being captured. They had followed the same road and suffered the same fate as our gun crew.

It was good to see old friends and we discussed how to escape. But my old enemy the interrogator reappeared, still shouting and raving, and bundled us all down into the air-raid shelter. There were about 40 of us by now, crammed into this dark dugout, and several were badly wounded and lay groaning all night. They posted two machine guns outside and that seemed to be that.

Corporal Alec Graham Pugh
Carrier Platoon, 2nd Battalion, Royal Warwickshire Regiment

And as a result, the battalion suffered heavy casualties including the commanding officer being killed, lost most of the vehicles and mortar guns etc. and failed to take the objective. And we withdrew to the outskirts of Benouville; the remains of the battalion gathered there and then reorganised and moved back to establish a defensive line about a mile from Lebisey, Lebisey Wood, in actual fact in Bieville itself.

Corporal Bill Bowdidge
9 Section Commander, 18 Platoon, D Company, 2nd Battalion, Royal Warwickshire Regiment

At Lebisey on the evening of D+1 I had a couple of mortar fragments in my arm. I reported to the MO the next morning & expected him to remove them there & then, but instead he pinned a label on me and I was sent back to the beach to board a TLS [LST] and taken back to Gosport & by train to Warwick Hosp. where I was visited by Brigadier Tomes, to whom I told of the death of Colonel Herdon. Regt.

14 Bannerman, *If I Don't Come Home, Letters from D-Day*, p.63.

HQ had not at that time been notified & he denied it, but came back the next day to say it was confirmed.

Captain Harry Illing
Officer Commanding A Company, 2nd Battalion Royal Warwickshire Regiment

Thus the first Battle of Lebisey was lost. It was galling that the great prize of Caen had so nearly fallen into our hands. Lebisey could in all probability have been captured if a properly coordinated attack had been put in instead of battalions being committed piecemeal: first a battalion on the evening of D-Day, secondly our own on the morning of D+1, and thirdly by another battalion on the evening of D+1. Even then it might still have succeeded if our attack had not gone off at half cock. It failed because the start line had not been secured and the attack went in without fire support. But in fairness to those who launched the attacks it must be remembered that it was not known that 21st Panzers had moved onto the feature, indeed information was to the contrary. Risks had to be taken in order to get on and establish as big a bridgehead as possible before German resistance hardened and their reserves could intervene.

The realities of war had hit many men hard, total battalion casualties killed, wounded and missing for Wednesday 7 June was 10 officers and 144 other ranks. Hailing from Stroud in Gloucestershire, Corporal Ron Nicholls was amongst those killed on D+1. Almost in sight of Caen, the advance had again been turned back giving more time for German reinforcement to arrive with *12. SS Panzerdivision Hitlerjugend* joining *21. Panzerdivision* at the front. For their steady leadership and bravery on 7 June, Major Kreyer, Major Bundock, Captain Illing and Sergeant Pittaway were recommended for decorations. Listed as missing presumed killed on 7 June 1944 was Private Albert 'Buck' Buckley; best friend of Private John Gundy, his body was never found, or at least when eventually found he was unidentifiable. Private John Gundy had been born 1920 in Birmingham, he was called up and enlisted on 20 June 1940 shortly after the Dunkirk evacuations and was a company runner for Major Ross but it would take more than 60 years for him to return to Normandy with the help of his wonderful granddaughters to pay his final respects to his friend.[15]

Private John Gundy
B Company, 2nd Battalion Royal Warwickshire Regiment

During the fighting and that, he (Buck) was in another company, you were scattered all over the place, everything was such a mess you know. We just said hello and good luck and all that, we were in different boats and that was it, I never saw him again.

15 Richardson, Deborah, *Finding Buck* http://www.youtube.com/watch?v=AbPGEBbWIoE

Captain Harry Illing
A Company, 2nd Battalion Royal Warwickshire Regiment

We had a rough time – but then we did not expect a picnic. Speaking for my own Company officers, NCOs and men, I can say they lived up to my highest hopes. Their discipline never lapsed. They fought like hell in a terrible situation. I was very proud to be allowed to command them. They were my friends and I loved them.... I do not think I shall ever know a better lot of chaps, or be in a battalion that could fight with greater guts.

Extract from *The Coventry Evening Telegraph*, Tuesday 11 July 1944

Warwickshire was strongly represented on the beach on D-Day when a British Infantry division was given the task for securing the left flank of the Allied force, the flank bounded by the Canal de Caen and the River Orne, writes a military correspondent.

The Royal Warwickshire Regiment was early on the beach, giving support where it was needed in the drive in – and after a heavy day's fighting they had an action all to themselves on D plus 1 (Wednesday, June 7) in Lebisey Wood.

Through this wood runs a road to Caen, and the point reached by the Royal Warwickshires was considerably in advance of the other troops in the British force.

It was known that the wood was occupied, but exact strength of the enemy had not been measured. Several companies of the regiment penetrated into the wood and came under heavy enemy fire. The enemy seemed to be all around them in strongly defended localities. Enemy tanks were there too. The anti-tank gun platoon of the Royal Warwickshires was ambushed. Many of the attacking troops spent 12 hours in the wood and were engaged in heavy fighting most of the time.

The Warwicks eventually withdrew, with casualties, to Biéville, which is also on the Caen road.

When I saw the Royal Warwickshires on the day after the engagement they were in good spirits and anxiously awaiting the chance of hitting back.

In 2022, after a campaign spearheaded by Jason Woods of the Royal Warwickshire Regiment Re-enactment Group, an outstanding memorial was unveiled near Lebisey, to honour men from the Royal Warwickshire Regiment who fought in Normandy in 1944.

6

Interlude

It was clear that the enemy could see the importance of Caen to the Allies, it being the main pivot point of their advance. By holding Caen for as long as possible, the Germans were guarding against any advance towards their naval base at Le Havre, the V Weapon sites in the Pas-de-Calais, and ultimately Paris. It was still widely believed within OKW that another landing was imminent, Patton's illusory 1st US Army Group was expected to land at the Pas-de-Calais, so it was also imperative to the Germans to prevent the Normandy force linking up with this second landing. The campaign of subterfuge and misinformation, Operation Fortitude as it was codenamed, is one of the great unsung victories of the Normandy campaign.

Captain Alastair J. M. Bannerman
Officer Commanding Anti-Tank Platoon, 2nd Battalion Royal Warwickshire Regiment

At dawn 8 June we were hauled out, and lined up and marched off with about five guards down the main road to Caen. We were very hungry, but it was good to be in the fresh air after that foul dugout.

We passed our burnt out carrier and another one of the Carrier Platoon. Soon we started to descend into Caen, and here we met an SS Panzer division lined up along the road, men and quite young boys in black who jeered and laughed at us. A far more vicious collection than the 21st Panzer regulars.

The city was unbelievably devastated and very few French were to be seen. We approached the centre past ruined churches and shells of houses, where we heard a growing hum, and about 20 Allied light bombers could be seen circling round towards the city. As the bombs started quite visibly to fall, gleaming in the sun, the German guards ran for shelter or flung themselves down. This was our chance. I shouted to Peter and Philip and to the nearest men, and we dashed off down a side street. The wall of a large building was slowly falling sideways, the bricks still clinging together, as we reached a square, but we turned sharply and missed the crash, and dashed on blindly. We ran suddenly into a group of gendarmes, and I gasped out that we were escaped prisoners. They immediately sprang into action, dramatically like the French, and with, "*Vite, vite, messieurs, dans le jardin,*" they rushed us into a ditch behind a public garden, where we fell panting. We ruffled up the grass again, and a few minutes later heard the guards running up questioning the gendarmes, who swore they had seen nothing, bless them.

We felt now that if we could be here for 24 hours we would be freed by the capture of Caen at any hour now. It had been our objective for the 6th or 7th, and we still hoped. Of course it was not taken until 3 months later. German guns and tanks moved by on the road as we lay within a stone's throw. The gendarmes returned twice with a bottle of Cognac, some biscuits and Camembert cheese. No one liked the Camembert except me, so I did well. There were 11 of us: 8 privates, Peter, Philip and I. We found we couldn't hope to move, as there was an open allotment behind us, the occupied road on our right and a filthy canal on our left, thick with mud and deep by the feel of a stick. A third visit was from a French man who arrived with a conspiratorial "psst," smashing flat all our elaborate camouflage of grass and twigs. He had two civilian suits and offered them to Peter and me, suggesting we should return to the cathedral crypt with him. A tempting offer, but we felt we couldn't leave the men, who knew no French or German, so regretfully we sent him away. The gendarmes came no more, and we got more and more depressed. The battlefront drew no nearer, and night came on. Our own shells started to land nearby, and a German gun replied from the road behind us. We could hear the orders quite clearly, and all night German vehicles moved past. We still had our helmets, which kept the splinters of our own shells off, but it had started to rain and it was a dismal, hungry, damp night we spent. We could think of no plan. It was miles now to our own troops, and we were right in the middle of Germans.

However, we had to do something, so before dawn we crept out and started to creep through the ruins. I felt if we could hit the racecourse we might get out into the country and join the *Maquis*, and soon re-join our army. But it was not to be. We were soon spotted, and, weaponless, we had to surrender once more.

The month following the first battle for Lebisey is widely ignored, even Marcus Cunliffe's wonderful history of the regiment gives little attention to it, however it is important to focus, even if briefly, on this period, as men of the regiment, real people, still worked and died there. On 8 June the whole of 185th Brigade formed a solid position with Biéville as the front line and Beauville as a reserve position. Under periodic shelling and even air attack, the three battalions dug in and began reorganising after the losses of the previous days. With such losses, notably with Captain Illing now in Morriston Hospital in Swansea and Lieutenant Adams at the Royal Victoria Hospital in East Grinstead, 2nd Warwicks was reorganised. Five officers and 123 ORs arrived from the regiment's first line reinforcements and a further 27 other ranks from the Worcestershire Regiment and four from the Dorsetshire Regiment were also drafted in as reinforcements. Lieutenant's D. A. Field, K. S. Taylor and J. Bindless were promoted to acting captain, with one new sergeant, eight new corporals and four new lance corporals in the ranks. One new officer, Canadian, Lieutenant D. J. Oland joined via the CANLOAN scheme.[1]

1 This scheme was created in 1944 to provide the British Army, running short of trained junior officers after nearly five years of war, with men from the Canadian Army with its abundance of readily available personnel.

Re-allocation of Battalion Officers – 8 June 1944

Battalion HQ	Maj. R. G. Kreyer – OC Maj. T. L. Brock – 2iC Capt. R. W. Heath – Adjutant Lt. P. W. F. Lamb – IO	**HQ Company**	Maj. T. L. Brock – OC Lt. J. R. Clarke – SO Lt. A. P. Roberts – TO Capt. S. J. Williams – QM Capt. J. H. T. Lawton (RAMC) – MO Capt. (Rev.) J. Austin (RACD) – Padre
A Company	Maj. M. Ryan – OC	Capt. M. L. B. Hall – 2iC	
Platoon Commanders	Lt. J. Erskine	Lt. O. W. Jarvis	
B Company	Maj. G. E. E. Ross – OC	Acting Capt. Lt. D. A. Field – 2iC	
Platoon Commanders	Lt. D. S. B. Roberts	Lt. A. J. W. Whitaker	Lt. D. R. Greenough
C Company	Capt. W. T. Barratt – OC	Acting Capt. K. A. Taylor – 2iC	
Platoon Commanders	Lt. R. M. McCrory	Lt. D. J .Oland (CANLOAN)	Lt. J. Martin-Webb
D Company	Maj. T. G. Bundock – OC	Capt. C. O. Blakey – 2iC	
Platoon Commanders	Lt. C. Briggs	Lt. E. E. Dentith	Lt. E. J. Bate
Support Company	Maj. G. F. J. Jerram – OC		
Carrier Platoon	**Mortar Platoon**	**Anti-Tank Platoon**	
Capt. ADR Smith – OC	Capt. F. Bell MM – OC	Acting Capt. J. Bindless – OC	

Private Ted Bedford
D Company, 2nd Battalion Royal Warwickshire Regiment

Shortly after.... we were ordered back to Beuville on the main road, passing Bieville where there was a long line of vehicles which had been attacked by Panzers earlier in the day.

On reaching Beuville we occupied a barn at a farm expecting a German counter-attack. Fortunately, this didn't happen.

Next morning, we were called to another barn nearby where two German prisoners were being held. They had managed to take one of our men as a hostage. We heard a shot and the body of the 2nd Battalion soldier was pushed out of the barn door. It was a foolish move on the part of the Germans since we were then able to put in an attack using phosphorous smoke grenades as well as rifle fire. Their bodies were found later after the barn had been burnt.

This event, what is in effect the murder of their guard by two PoWs, recounted by Private Bedford 60 years later,[2] is not mentioned (as you might expect) in the official Regimental History or in the Battalion War Diary written at the time. It would appear to relate to either 8 June or 9 June, which if accurate may indicate the tragic circumstances of the death of Private Herbert Martin, the son of Herbert and Mary Ann Martin, of Dordon in Warwickshire, his headstone in Douvres Le Délivrande Commonwealth War Graves Cemetery reads:

> IN LOVING MEMORY OF OUR DEAR SON WHO DIED THAT WE MIGHT LIVE. GONE BUT NOT FORGOTTEN

The Battalion was placed in a rota with the 2nd KSLI, switching between the front line at Biéville and then five days in reserve at Beuville. 2nd Warwicks took the opportunity to consolidate in reserve, however this was no rest period; on 9 June, Captain Field of A Company, led a successful patrol to the start line of the attack on Lebisey Wood to recover equipment that had been left behind, while also taking five German soldiers as prisoners, who were promptly sent back to HQ. It was rumoured that German snipers were still in the Beuville area, so a D Company patrol searched the village houses, but no trace of said snipers was found. On 10 June the battalion moved forward to Biéville to take over the position left by 2nd KSLI as they headed back. They were sporadically shelled during the day, but Major General Rennie DSO MBE was still able to visit the battalion.

Private Ted Bedford
D Company, 2nd Battalion Royal Warwickshire Regiment

> For the first four days after landing we had no food and only water from the village pump at Beuville. Our emergency rations were still with our equipment which we had to abandon prior to the attack on the ridge at Lebisey.
>
> Over the next few days, within the grounds of the farm, we were continually under fire from snipers and look several casualties. We were also attacked by a low level bomber which dropped several bombs among us.
>
> We became really fed up with all the sniping, so seven of us volunteered to try to flush out the enemy. We made our way through the main street of Beuville searching for snipers, three men on each side of the road, hugging the shadows of the houses, and myself walking down the middle of the street making some noise to attract the snipers! We went down the street and back again.... but there was no sign of the enemy.
>
> A couple of days later the whole unit conducted a thorough house by house, building by building search of the village but found no enemy, although we were still receiving sniper fire.
>
> We were very surprised when a lone German appeared at the farm seeking to surrender. He told us he had several comrades who also wanted to surrender

2 *The Antelope, The Journal of The Royal Warwickshire Regiment.* (2005 Edition)

but sought assurances that they would be well treated, especially since two were wounded.

We assured him that they would be treated in accordance with the Geneva Convention. A few minutes later he returned with half-a-dozen comrades and we took them prisoner. The sniping ceased.

Major T. L. Brock
HQ Company, 2nd Battalion Royal Warwickshire Regiment

We remained at Beuville until 10 June when we relieved 2nd KSLI at Biéville. During our stay at Biéville we were subjected to sporadic shell fire, and one bombing attack, and suffered a few casualties. Our position was rather compromised by the presence of a field artillery regiment just behind our positions, and no doubt we took a lot of punishment intended for the guns.

Sergeant Bob Barnett (Intelligence Sergeant)
B Company, 2nd Battalion Royal Warwickshire Regiment

During the period when we were facing the Germans and they were facing us, in the month before we actually took Lebisey, we were largely based at a village called Biéville, the front line was towards the bottom end of the village. Of course, it wasn't a sort of solid front line in the First World War sense, it was a series of strong points, and the Germans would come up in the night and come quite close and actually into parts of the village.

Between 10 and 15 June, 2nd Warwicks remained in Biéville, amidst an unpleasant mixture of shelling and night patrols, with its constant flow of casualties. However, on the 11th the new CO arrived, Lieutenant Colonel Denis Lucius Alban Gibbs DSO, formally of the Queen's Royal Regiment; with Major Kreyer returning to his role as second in command. Lieutenant Colonel Gibbs had commanded 1/6th Battalion Queen's Royal Regiment in North Africa, where he had been awarded the DSO, however during the Battle of El Alamein he had been taken prisoner and subsequently incarcerated in Italy. In 1943 he escaped from the PoW Camp he was held in, and for the next 53 days and over 1,000km, he led a group of fellow escapees to Allied lines and freedom.

The same day, it was felt that the Germans might be withdrawing from Lebisey Woods, and D Company provided a fighting patrol to test this possibility, unfortunately the woods were still very much strongly held and the patrol returned quickly with their casualties. Lieutenant Briggs of 18th platoon, D Company was injured on the 12th and during the 13th the carrier platoon made a patrol to a small woodland just south of Biéville, designated Square 0473, finding it clear of enemy.

Private Dennis Pettitt
D Company, 2nd Battalion Royal Warwickshire Regiment

> Where he [Topper Brown] actually did me a favour, was when we had to go out on patrol, you could do a fighting patrol, at night, nobody liked them because they were full of danger, so we went out with Sergeant Geddes, nice bloke Sergeant Geddes, and we went out to do our 24 hours behind this hedgerow listening and observing and all of a sudden I heard a crack of a rifle and little twigs of the hedgerow fell on us, two minutes later crack, more leaves falling over us and.... I said to Fred Geddes, somebody is trying to tell us something and I think we ought to bugger off, because nobody is going to fire over our heads when they could get all of us, so it ain't a German. He says alright so he crept along and up the other hedgerow. We got back to base and Topper was there and he said what the bloody hell were you hanging about for, there were 12 or 20 bloody SS bloody machine gunners the other side of the hedge!

On the same day Major General Rennie was wounded in action, and shortly after replaced by Major General L. G. Whistler GCB KBE DSO. Lieutenant McCrory was wounded when C Company, with Charlie Tweed, was shelled by a 'moaning minnie,' as the infamous German six barrelled rocket launchers, *Nebelwerfers*, were known. Anti-tank and anti-personnel mines were laid in front of their positions on 14 June and after heavier shelling than usual, fighting patrols were sent out that night, with one exchanging fire with a German position on the outskirts of Lebisey Wood. While being relieved on the 15th, Lieutenant Bate of D Company was wounded. With 2nd KSLI now back in Biéville the battalion returned to Beauville to be joined by 39 reinforcements from the Royal Welsh Fusiliers.

Sergeant Bob Barnett (Intelligence Sergeant)
B Company, 2nd Battalion Royal Warwickshire Regiment

> It was a strange situation; when it was quiet, it was deathly quiet, because there were no birds or anything, the trees were all bare, a bit like the First World War scenes that you see in films, but then occasionally either side would open out and open up all the guns for about five minutes, we used to call it a hate, a five-minute hate. Another strange thing was that the civilians were still there in the village because we were still so close to the coast, there was nowhere they could be evacuated. And I always remember the mayor one day gave me a box of Camembert cheese, which was a great treasure. The only trouble was he'd had it so long it apparently smelled to high heaven. Although I've got no sense of smell, the other lads in the section had.... and they wouldn't have this cheese in the hole with us and I had to keep it under a hedge and nip out when I wanted to get at it.

The period 15 to 21 June was a much quieter affair for the battalion, interrupted only by occasional shelling. Three German soldiers surrendered to the forward company on the 16th and Lieutenant Lamb, the intelligence officer, took a patrol out into the valley between Biéville and Lebisey, to assess possible crossing points for any future plans to attack Lebisey. Miraculously on the same day, Private Sutcliffe A Company, who had been wounded on 7 June and survived on rations taken from the dead in the woodland outside Lebisey, finally made his way back to battalion lines and was evacuated.[3] The remaining troops and vehicles of the battalion arrived from the UK on the 18th, another 50 ORs and 16 vehicles. As a sign of what was to come, Lieutenant Colonel Gibbs DSO, Captain Barratt, Major Bundock and B Squadron commander from Staffordshire Yeomanry made a reconnaissance trip through the valley to Lebisey on 19 June, to assess options for the eventual attack. On the same day, Charlie Tweed penned the following letter to his sister Jessie, at home in Atherstone:

> Dear Jess,
> Just a few lines in answer to your most welcome letter which I've received. I hope they find you in the best of health as they say at present. I knew my letters were held up Jess but I didn't think it would take a fortnight to get to you. Well, when you wrote this letter you didn't know that I was in France or not for sure, but I was in France two days before you wrote this. You see our Division was the first to land in our sector of the Beaches and we had a very rough time of it for the first three days. It's not anything like that at present what with Jerry's mortars and artillery bombing around the area and ours doing the same only worse to him all day, then they go on through the night against the two Air Forces the RAF and Luftwaffe. So, you can see it isn't what the papers describe as all quiet at the front Jess. Thanks for wishing me luck Jess and don't worry I'm alright. I'm down dug into a trench writing this letter and as long as I can write to you all at home, I'm happy. I've received three letters from Joan, from mother and one from you today so I've had lots to read and write Jess, and it's kept my mind off the war for a bit. I'm a bit cramped up and my writing isn't much good so I hope you'll excuse it a bit Jess. No, I don't think you ignored my letter Jess, I didn't expect to get my mail soon in France anyway. Well as I've already said I was with the first to land, and as you can see by the papers we did a good job and made it possible for the second wave of troops to land without any opposition Jess, and now we're firmly dug in well inland and right out in the front waiting for the word to go so that we can start our second big battle. The first was severe and we lost a lot of our Batt. but Jerry lost more than we did and there's still dozens lying dead on the place where we fought that haven't been buried yet Jess so we are not doing too bad for a start, but wait until we start the big push and then keep your eye on the map and watch the bridgehead start to push inland again. We're only stopping a moment for a breath of air Jess. Well Cal sent me a 4/- P.O. Jess but I don't know when I shall be able to spend it out here and he was a fool to send it because I gave those things to him. Say, you will have to thank him from me Jess and now I think that is all I can say at present Jess so remember me to Cal and Ron and I will close now.
>
> So cheerio and God Bless you all Jess, Cal and Ron
> From Your Loving Brother Charlie xxxxxxx
> Xxxxxxxxxxxxxxxxxxxx

3 TNA WO 171/1387, '2nd Battalion, the Royal Warwickshire Regiment, War Diary,' June 1944.

As intelligence sergeant, Bob Barnett could speak French and was a useful man to have around, he acted as interpreter for colleagues as well as having his own duties and he was quickly making friends with the locals.

Sergeant Bob Barnett (Intelligence Sergeant)
B Company, 2nd Battalion Royal Warwickshire Regiment

> In the village, there was one man in particular, he was a student from Caen University named Phillipe, and he used to come and talk to me a lot, he used to bring me a lot of information, and he also made sure the civilians still there were treated properly, one day he asked me if I could help an old man who was sick and he took me to a farm, where there was big barn with a sort of semi underground section to it and the women and the children and the old people of the village were all living down this semi underground place and I took the motorbike.... I managed to get him back down to the coast and he got some medical treatment there...

With the next switch between 2nd KSLI and 2nd Warwicks taking place, a C Company platoon made a standing patrol and occupied the woodland of Square 0473 again, the patrols were scheduled to rotate every 24 hours. The previously mentioned Captain Batt returned to the battalion on 22 June, returning to his role as adjutant, a position held for the 1st Battalion in 1912 by Monty himself. Captain Heath was appointed second in command of D Company as Captain Blakey departed to take up the mantle as GSO III. Major General Whistler visited the battalion on 23 June. The Divisional GOC was a well-liked officer, known as either 'Bolo Whistler,' due to his service against the Bolshevik forces in 1919 with the British garrison at Archangel; or 'Private Bolo,' due to his easy rapport with the so-called common man of the other ranks. Even on the day of the General's visit casualties continued to be suffered, two of the casualties, both reported KIA on 23 June, were Private Lawrence Frank Drake and Private George Albert Brueton. Private Brueton, from Small Heath, Birmingham; son of Alfred and Laura, was a pre-war regular, joining up at just 18 years of age on 16 January 1939. Posted to France with the battalion with the BEF on 23 September 1939,[4] he was ultimately evacuated on 31 May 1940 from Bray Dunes, Dunkirk with those of the 2nd Battalion who remained. His service records show the date that George was KIA as 23rd, but the headstone and Grave Registration report state 25th. Jason Woods, a relative of George Brueton has researched extensively and it is possible that he was killed 23 June, the Battalion War Diary for that day simply states: "Usual Patrols and rather heavy shelling. Some casualties," but they were not recovered, and thus his death was not registered until the 25th.

There were a number of patrols out on 25 June, both British and German. The carrier platoon clashed with an enemy patrol taking casualties while trying to make contact with C Company at Square 0473. Then C Company themselves were heavily mortared in the woodland position. On the morning of the 26th, two Polish deserters from the troops defending Lebisey Wood surrendered to A Company, before 2nd KSLI

4 Jason Woods and Royal Warwickshire Regiment Re-enactment Facebook Group.

remanned the positions in Biéville, with 2nd Warwicks moving back to Beuville and the wonderful news that they would be sending their first party to the corps rest centre. Fortunately, due to Bob's friendship, there were lighter moments within the greater turmoil of war, with one man demonstrating his less martial skills.

Sergeant Bob Barnett (Intelligence Sergeant)
B Company, 2nd Battalion Royal Warwickshire Regiment

> Phillipe, Marcel and Solange lived.... at a small chateau on the edge of the village.... they had down at the house.... a grand piano, and Jimmy Baldwin our corporal, was one of those people who can play anything by ear or music and one day he.... gave us a little recital.... Piano or string base, he was very talented.

Across 27th and 28th the mobile bath unit arrived with all ranks able to enjoy their first true wash since leaving the UK. However, there was also heavy shelling on both days with a number of officers and men becoming casualties; Lieutenant Greenhough and five ORs from B Company amongst them. The German radio station, *Deutschlandsender* announced on 28 June that Alastair Bannerman, Captain Pike, Captain Waterworth and Lieutenant Healey were indeed prisoners of the Third Reich, a great relief for all as they were simply listed MIA until that point. It is also important to acknowledge the arrival of 1/7th Battalion Royal Warwickshire Regiment in Normandy from Newhaven on 28 June. 1/7th Warwicks were commanded by Lieutenant Colonel E. J. Jerram MC, previously of the 2/7th Battalion. 1/7th Warwicks were part of 197th Infantry Brigade, 59th Division and had their own roles in the battles to come.

Captain Alastair JM Bannerman
OC Anti-Tank Platoon, 2nd Battalion Royal Warwickshire Regiment

> And so began the frustrating business of being 'in the bag.' A night at Le Bourget and then by train to Châlons sur Marne, with its systematic starvation and solitary confinement to coax and cudgel information from us. The commandant looked like Dracula, with a white face and long bat-like cloak. Then Hadamar, our first stop in Germany, and so finally by cattle truck, and all its slow miseries of endless halts and little food, to Brunswick and Oflag 79.

Heavy shelling continued periodically over the next two days, especially on the battalions' forward positions. Unexpectedly, at around 0700 hours on 30 June, two ME109s strafed the rear echelon area which even though it did not cause any damage, was a shock. A hundred men from B & D Companies were ordered to lay mines during the night, with cover from a C Company platoon.

For the whole period 8–30 June the battalion's total casualties amounted to 16 officers and 245 other ranks. Of this, 2 officers and 27 ORs were evacuated due to illness or general injury – even in war accidents happen and people fall sick.

German reinforcement divisions continued to become available, however they were understrength and rushed into attack piecemeal instead of waiting to build-up in strength first. Possibly the greatest disadvantage the Germans faced was air power, with the Luftwaffe almost entirely absent, the Allied air forces reigned supreme. Any enemy troops sighted or convoys moving into position and supplies and reinforcements coming by train from the Fatherland, were almost immediately assailed by Allied fighters, and most memorably for those on the receiving end, the rocket-firing Typhoons. For any larger formations sighted, the ever-present navy anchored off the coast were called upon to provide devastating strikes.

***Major* Hans von Luck**
Panzergrenadierregiment Nr 125

> ...any movement on the battlefield, even of an individual vehicle, the enemy reacted with concentrated fire from the navy or attacks by fighter-bombers. Either our radio communications were being intercepted or the navy had divided up the whole area into grid squares and had only to pass on the square number to launch a sudden concentration of fire. Against such concentrations, and for the night, we all dug foxholes beside our vehicles, which provided some protection. All our supplies came from the Paris area and could be moved only by night.

7

Charnwood

As the month changed, so did the troops' workload, for July would see renewed efforts to take Caen and breakout from the bridgehead that had been held since 6 June. Pressure was building on Monty from all quarters, the British public wanted decisive victories to celebrate after nearly five years of war, Churchill and Eisenhower expected action and the RAF clamoured for advancement to capture ground beyond Caen that could be used for airfields. Above all Monty could see the British star waning. British reinforcement numbers dwindled as the available male labour pool was almost dry, but US troops, whole divisions, continued to pour into France at a rate the British could not keep pace with. The US was swiftly becoming the dominant partner in the Allied organisation and Monty did not want to cede power to anybody. As it was, the American advance from the Utah and Omaha bridgeheads was floundering, and it was down to the Canadians and British to draw as many enemy divisions as possible into battle around Caen to provide relief for the US Forces. This also allowed Monty to focus on his original D-Day objective, taking the Norman Capital, seat of William the Conqueror, once and for all. The Canadian 3rd Infantry Division would attack Carpiquet on 4 July in advance of the main assault. Then, on 8 July, the British 3rd and 59th Infantry Divisions[1] supported by the 79th Armoured Division under Major General Percy ('Hobo') Hobart, as well as the Canadian Troops involved earlier, would launch the next assault. They faced *21. Panzerdivision*, *12. SS Panzerdivision 'Hitlerjugend'*, now led by General Kurt 'Panzer Meyer', which included elements of *SS-Panzergrenadierregimenter Nr 25* and *Nr 26*, plus elements of 1. *SS-Panzergrenadierregiment* and the recently arrived *Luftwaffen Feld Division Nr 16,* very few troops however, were stationed in the city of Caen itself.

The 2nd Warwicks, still in Beuville at the beginning of July, continued to suffer occasional casualties under sporadic shellfire and periodically mounting patrols as required, during one of which, on 2 July. Lance Corporal Arthur Henry Boswell, 24 years old and from Warwick, was killed. On the first day of the month the Staffordshire Yeomanry hosted the battalion's company and platoon commanders to improve combined arms close-country operations, with Brigadier Prior-Palmer (CO 27th Armoured Brigade) particularly focusing on cooperation with Crocodiles and AVREs. However, while this

1 Including 1/7th Battalion, the Royal Warwickshire Regiment.

was taking place, 20 ORs we released to visit the cinema back in Lion-sur-Mer. Even more appreciated, the following day the battalion was visited by the mobile bath unit again. Also, on 2 July Brigadier K. P. Smith was replaced as OC 185th Brigade by Brigadier Eric Bols. Smith has not been judged kindly following the decisions made on 6 & 7 June, but is that fair? Were the decisions he made the only ones that were available to him at the time?

On 3 July, 2nd Warwicks returned to Biéville relieving 2nd KSLI from their front line duties, and immediately set about preparing patrols to take place the following day. During a 4 July patrol it was discovered that *21. Panzerdivision* had also been relieved and had been replaced in Lebisey by elements of *16. Luftwaffen Feld Division*. The 16th had only recently transferred from The Netherlands, and most of the division was either still there, or in transit to Normandy, thus it was a depleted force in position in Lebisey, around 500 largely untried men. On 5 July, Brigade issued orders detailing the renewed assault on Lebisey Wood – Operation Charnwood, with 8 July as D-Day. On the moonlit night of 6 July, Lieutenant C. W. Jarvis led a patrol to the very edge of Lebisey Wood without being fired upon, but he finally pushed just too far and two casualties were sustained when the German defenders hurled grenades at the patrol.

Major T. L. Brock
HQ Company, 2nd Battalion Royal Warwickshire Regiment

> Some splendid work was done by patrol leaders and some had extremely narrow escapes. In particular, a patrol lead by Captain C. W. Jarvis penetrated the forward enemy positions and eventually bumped an enemy post, which opened fire. Captain Jarvis was hit by a grenade which bounced off him and exploded on the ground.[2]

Incredibly, the Battalion War Diary excludes the actions of Sergeant Jennings during these patrols (perhaps because of his rank?) which saw him awarded the Military Medal, it was presumably Lieutenant Jarvis who successfully recommended Sergeant Jennings for this award. The below extract from *The London Gazette* dated 20 March 1945, best describes his actions:

> Sergeant Jennings has led his platoon on patrol against the enemy and has at all times displayed outstanding courage and devotion to duty, qualities which have been reflected in the efficiency of the men under his command. During the concentration of the 3rd Division at Lebisey it became essential to discover the precise position of the enemy prior to an attack being made. On 6 July 1944, Sergeant Jennings led a patrol detailed to go to Lebisey Wood. Leading his men in a wide detour through enemy held territory, Sergeant Jennings approached his objective from the flank unobserved.
>
> As the first building entered by the patrol showed signs of recent occupation. Sergeant Jennings went on to the next farm where the enemy was encountered in

2 At the point of time in question, Jarvis was serving as a Lieutenant. He was not actually promoted to Acting Captain until 17 August 1944.

> great strength. The patrol was attacked with grenades and automatics. During the attack a German sentry was killed and other casualties inflicted on the enemy. Sergeant Jennings, realising that at least one member of his patrol must get back and report the position, directed covering fire onto the farm and thus enabled the rest of the patrol to withdraw to a neighbouring wood. Although enemy machine guns were now in action, Sergeant Jennings continued to provide covering fire until his man were out of danger and then withdrew himself, the patrol returned without a casualty.
>
> The courage of this NCO in risking his life many times to cover the withdrawal of the men under his command serves as an example to all ranks.

The same evening and early hours of the following day, RE and 2nd Warwicks' pioneers removed the minefields that lay in the path of the soon to be attacking forces. Lieutenant Colonel Gibbs DSO issued the final orders for Operation Charnwood on 7 July, which would be preceded that night by 467 RAF Halifax and Lancaster bombers pulverising a 1km by 4km section of Northern Caen. With the distinctive throb of the Avro Lancaster's Rolls-Royce Merlin engines and the hum of the Handley Page Halifax bomber's Bristol Hercules radial engines assaulting their ears, the men of 2nd Warwicks stood amazed at the air fleet passing over their heads.

Major Raymond Birt
22nd Dragoons

> From the edges of the sky to the hedges nearby, the world was rocking and shaking with noise and the flash of guns. Our RHQ armoured cars were shaken by the hot blast of roadside batteries. Soon a thick fog of smoke settled down across the fields in the still morning air, and the crack of the guns merged into a steady beat of exhausting power and authority.

Inexplicably, due to RAF concerns over 'creep back' the bomb line had been set at almost 5,500m (technically 6,000yds) ahead of the Allied start line. Meaning that with little more than an SS canteen company in the city, French civilians would feel the full force of the RAF and not the defenders facing 2nd Warwicks and the Allies. What is worse, is that the raid took place on the evening of 7 July, taking off from their UK airfields at 2030 hours and crossing the Channel before releasing their deadly load of 500lbs and 1,000lbs incendiary and high explosive bombs, 2,560 tons in total, many hours in advance of the ground forces' H-Hour, which allowed the defenders time to recover and regroup. It would be the responsibly of the divisional and corps artillery to bombard the untouched ground in front of the Allied start line.

Flight Sergeant Francis McGovern
Halifax Bomber 426 (RCAF) Squadron, No. 6 (RCAF) Group, Bomber Command

> We made an attack on Caen in support of the invasion forces, and I think we were much criticised afterwards for the mess that we made, in so far that we took out the target all right – which we were told at the time was a steelworks on the banks of

> a canal, which the Germans had fortified quite heavily with anti-aircraft weapons, and weapons of one kind and another – and were making life quite difficult for the army and their advance. However, we took the place out, and from what I recall of it we simply left quite appalling clouds of dust and smoke in our wake, and the army were then complaining that we made life even more difficult because the roads that they'd intended to follow were simply strewn with rubble and all sorts of rubbish.

This show of airpower was not a relief for all, many hundreds of French civilians, including children and the nuns of the city's many convents and religious institutions were killed during this raid, leading BBC War Correspondent, Frank Gillard, to compare it to the murder of a city: 'My own feeling about the bombing was that it was really unnecessary.... an act of sheer frustration on the part of the higher command.'[3] The once beautiful city had been pulverised. Consequently, the raid left its streets blocked and strewn with rubble from the ancient buildings, meaning that it was very difficult, if not impossible, for Allied armoured formations and vehicles to pass through the city as planned. Even before the Charnwood bombing offensive, Captain Bannerman, after being captured and transported through the city, had witnessed first-hand the destruction already wrought upon Caen and the effect it had on French civilians.

Captain Alastair J. M. Bannerman
Officer Commanding Anti-Tank Platoon, 2nd Battalion Royal Warwickshire Regiment (Prisoner of War)

> We waited beside the road, while refugees poured out of the ruined and smoking city. These pathetic people, carrying the bundles that we all recognise from so many newsreels, shuffled by endlessly. Some looked at us curiously, others apathetically, while others, perhaps to gain German favour, spat at us and called, "*Cochon, salaud.*" It was understandable after the non-stop destruction of their once lovely old city.
>
> In addition to the heavy bombers pounding the defenders around Caen, there was the constant and supposedly reassuring presence of low level air support, as 185th Brigade discovered only too well.

Lieutenant Dennis 'Dingy' Bell
Carrier Platoon, 1st Battalion Royal Norfolk Regiment

> Later in the morning I was approaching Lebisey, by the track leading up from the Beauregard Road to the left hand front corner of the wood, when I experienced a little friendly bombing by two of our own planes – they had obviously mistaken me for the Hun.

3 Andrew Williams, *D-Day to Berlin* (London: Hodder & Stoughton, 2004), p.131.

Captain John Talbot MC
16th Field Battery Royal Artillery

> On the final assault on Caen on 8 July I was the FOO [Forward Observation Officer] in my Sherman tank (it had a wooden gun! – to accommodate an extra wireless set!) with the Staffordshire Yeomanry in a sweep east of Lebisey Wood. After being bombed by some American aircraft we rounded the wood.... moved on to the high ground overlooking Caen itself.

It is perhaps not surprising that variations of, 'When the RAF bomb, the Germans duck; when the Germans bomb, the British duck, but whenever the Americans bomb, both sides duck' became common among front line troops.

Copies of the Battalion Operational Orders for Operation Charnwood from 6 July still exist, although they rather confusingly refer to it as Operation Sherwood, presumably an error on the part of the typist. They include fantastic levels of detail including hand drawn maps, location code names, artillery programme and a wonderful illustration of the battalion communication lines. The plan called for 185th Brigade to retake Lebisey Wood, with 2nd Warwicks taking the right of the advance, 1st Norfolks the left, and 2nd KSLI in reserve ready to pass through the leading battalions once Lebisey had been captured. Divisional support under command of 2nd Warwicks for the attack would be one platoon of 17th Field Company RE, B Squadron of the Staffordshire Yeomanry, the SPs of 21st Anti-Tank Battery RA and one section from 223rd Field Ambulance.

Everything for the battalion since 7 June had focused on Lebisey Wood. Two companies would lead the assault, with C Company to the left and D Company the right (Party X), the two remaining companies would follow up, A Company to the left and B Company to the right (Party Y). In the early hours, following the white tape lines laid by the mine clearing parties, all 185th Brigade troops took up their positions prior to H-Hour, with 2nd Warwicks' leading companies reaching their start line a few hundred metres from the northern edge of the woods, at 0430 hours, just as the corps artillery began its own barrage.

Shortly afterwards, the companies received heavy fire from the Luftwaffe ground troops defending the Wood, with the reserve companies quickly sustaining casualties. With the artillery's rolling barrage moving forward, the leading companies, without armoured support, advanced so quickly in the wake of the destruction, that the defenders had been unable to rally themselves as the barrage moved on, and they were quickly dealt with. With one squadron from the East Riding Yeomanry offering additional protection on the right flank, the advance continued apace with many small pockets of defenders being left to be taken care of by the reserve companies and two troops of the Staffordshire Yeomanry, that had finally overcome a difficult passage over a tank obstacle blocking their path. Captain W. T. Barratt's C Company and D Company led by Tom Bundock took their primary objective on the southern edge of Lebisey Wood by 0600 hours while the defenders came to life and began a heavy artillery and mortar attack on the wood itself with their former positions as prearranged targets, as the two follow up companies moved forward.

Sergeant Major Russell King
C Company, 2nd Battalion Royal Warwickshire Regiment

We had a massive barrage and we followed the barrage up I remember, we were right behind the barrage, of our own artillery and I remember thinking, all the lads in fact I suppose were thinking there cannot be any Germans left after this lot, but by God they were, we really got hammered, C Company really got hammered as far as that action was concerned, and I remember getting wounded, now where it was following the barrage up, because we were really close to the barrage, whether it was one that had fallen short and went off I don't know, but anyway I got hit in the hand, actually the arm and hand.... I didn't even know, and I thought bloody hell my arms gone queer, when I look down I'm all bloody blood, I thought oh hell I must have got hit and I just made my way back to the first aid post.... just back down the hill.

Private Geoffrey Duncan
B Company, 1st Battalion Royal Norfolk Regiment

...the barrage was lifted to enable us to enter the wood and root out the defenders, we had only gone a few yards when we found ourselves on the wrong end of a German counter barrage of mortars and field artillery which was firing air burst shells, the red hot shrapnel sprayed down...

Captain W. J. Phillips
Intelligence Officer, 1/7th Battalion Royal Warwickshire Regiment

...a great swathe had been cut in the standing corn, clearing a field of fire for a machine gun position which appeared as no more than a slight mound among the stubble. Between the machine gun and the corn, the open field... was strewn with tripwire grenades. Barbed wire lined the edge of the crops where our riflemen emerged into the open...

The variety of tank support once again came to the fore; in addition to the two troops[4] of Sherman tanks alongside D Company, there were two troops of mine clearing flail tanks, one troop of AVREs and a troop of the terrifying flamethrower Crocodiles in close support should their specialist skills be required.[5]

A Wolverine M10 Tank Destroyer came to the aid of one A Company platoon that had become embroiled in a veritable rabbit warren of an enemy command post that morning; it was quickly destroyed thanks to the Wolverine's 3-inch (76.2mm) gun. Lieutenant D. S. B. Roberts led his platoon into the village of Lebisey, quickly clearing a significant area for the platoons behind to reinforce. By 1145 hours, encountering little enemy fire, A Company, now commanded by Major M. Ryan, with the assistance of the

4 A troop generally consisting of three M4 Sherman's with 75mm armament and one supporting Sherman Firefly with a 17-pdr gun.
5 This may seem like a lot of tanks but it IS what the Operation Orders state.

battalion carriers had pushed ahead and taken Point X-Ray, the section of high ground overlooking Caen around 1,000m to the south of Lebisey Wood.

Major Robin Kreyer DSO
Second in Command, 2nd Battalion Royal Warwickshire Regiment

> ...the Bn captured the position in Lebisey which had caused us a lot of trouble on D+1 and had been holding up our advance for so long.
>
> 'C' and 'D' Coys were the forward Coys for this attack and took their objectives behind a tremendous artillery barrage, with 'A' and 'B' Coys mopping up behind. Then 'A' Coy advanced a further 800 yards and held on to some high ground under very heavy mortar fire until relieved by another Bn.
>
> Bill Barrett, cmdg 'C' Coy was knocked unconscious by a piece of shell in the back of the neck but came to very quickly when he found one of his sergeants taking his watch and weapons off him thinking he was dead, and carried on with his Coy.

Once settled onto their new position, A Company came under heavy fire from the dreaded 'moaning minnies' positioned ahead of them. With their exploitation objective successfully taken, sufficient cover had been found or created and Ryan's men were able to hold the ground until 2nd KSLI came through their position at 1500 hours in their own stage of the advance. With the regimental aid post established at Chateaux Beiville, and the casualty clearing station following behind the advancing troops, the stretcher-bearers and field ambulances tending to the men of 2nd Warwicks were amongst the hardest pressed soldiers and bore witness to the resulting horrors.

Nursing Orderly First Class Jim Wisewell
223rd Field Ambulance Royal Army Medical Corps

> As the day wore on, sunny and scorching hot, the tide of casualties rose. Dozens and dozens were carried in. Our treatment centre always had 3 on the trestles being attended to and soon the approaches were lined with a queue. Hour after hour we worked and evacuated, and still the flow continued. Ghastly wounds there were, of every type and state of severity. Heads with skulls so badly smashed the bone and brain and pillow were almost indivisible; faces with horrible lacerations; jaws blown completely away leaving only two sad eyes to plead for relief from pain. Chests pierced through with shrapnel and lungs that spouted blood from gushing holes. Arms were mangled into shapeless masses left hanging by muscle alone and waiting the amputation knife.

The men were now allowed a moment to reorganise themselves and take up defensive positions in accordance with the Phase III Battalion Orders. A & D Companies occupied the crossroads and a series of houses in Lebisey village, B Company were allotted a north-westerly corner of Lebisey Woods, and C Company occupied the orchards and the water tower and its surrounding houses. The Anti-Tank Platoon with four 6-pdrs, were to follow behind the advance to cover the southern and western approaches to

Lebisey Wood in support of C Company and B Company areas, and 41st Anti-Tank Battery RA coming up to support the area occupied by D Company. Finally, a rudimentary protective minefield was laid by all companies, which would be built up further upon the arrival of RE teams.

Corporal Alec Graham Pugh
Carrier Platoon, 2nd Battalion, Royal Warwickshire Regiment

> Well there was only the odd burst of fire that I could hear because all resistance had crumbled, and some prisoners were taken.... The first two companies stopped and occupied Lebisey Wood, consolidated there and the two companies that we were flanking carried on through the wood and over the open ground, and the tanks followed behind. Well, there they got to the open ground, they moved in front of us some of the tanks, because we could look to our left and see across. And unfortunately, there was either German Tiger tanks with 88s mounted or an 88 gun dug in on the right and they promptly proceeded to polish off these tanks one after the other, the few that was left were forced to withdraw back a bit because they were right on the skyline.

With a heavy heart but their objectives taken, the men of the battalion were able to now take the opportunity to finally recover the bodies of their friends and comrades lost in these woods on 7 June, which must have been a harrowing experience after their being exposed to repeated bombardments and the heat and elements of a French summer for a month. The strength and conviction of the padre, Captain J. Austin, were once more called upon to give these men the final respects denied to them in death, as well as supporting those who remained. Those that could not be identified were eventually buried with the simple headstone reading 'A Soldier of the 1939–45 War.'

Lieutenant Colonel D. L. A. Gibbs DSO
Officer Commanding 2nd Battalion Royal Warwickshire Regiment

> ...we have had a most successful battle, for which the Bn. has earned high praise, and which avenged the sad set back on D+1. I do not think I have ever seen such gallant high heartedness both on the eve of battle and on capture of the objective, in any troops, anywhere. The Regt could not be more highly spoken of than it is being spoken of at the moment, by those who know what they are speaking about!

The task set for 2nd Warwicks and 185th Brigade was just one facet of Operation Charnwood, not all objectives were taken on 8 July, but Charnwood is viewed as a success despite a strong fighting rearguard the northern portion of Caen, up to the river, was now in Allied hands, and the vital airfield at Carpiquet had finally been taken by the Canadians after their earlier frustrations.

Corporal Alec Graham Pugh
Carrier Platoon, 2nd Battalion, Royal Warwickshire Regiment

> We had been told, that when we got past Lebisey Wood, on the right there was a village…. and the way leading into this village was a sunken road. They said that before we got there, the 25 pounders would put down a concentrated fire for so many minutes and then lift for us to go in. Well the rifle companies went in before that and there was no fire come down, and they captured 90 Germans. There was all sorts of milling around the village and we had pulled up in this sunken road…. And this concentrated fire came down on us from our own 25 pounders. I don't know what had gone wrong, whether we'd moved too quickly or there was any misunderstanding. And we lay in like a little ditch in this sunken road, but the poor old rifle company blokes, some were having to get in slit trenches which the Germans had dug and the Germans were lying there and the rifle company blokes and of course they were taking the brunt of this barrage. And the Germans joined in with *minenwerfers*, the six barrelled mortar. Didn't last too long, but the damage was done then… and of course the poor old Germans had already undergone an horrific bombardment by air and artillery, and they were in no state, they were all bomb happy, a bundle of nerves.
>
> And we remained there… well we remained across the sky line from the village right across this ridge, we took up position and the wounded was removed and the German prisoners sent back. And the Royal Ulster Rifles then moved through us to continue down the open ground into Caen. And it was rather strange because that was my birthday, 9 July.

Despite the success, the battalion had once more paid a heavy price under the leaves of Lebisey Wood; 26 men had been killed, including Lance Corporal Alfred Russell and the Canadian Captain Cohen; 99 wounded including Captains Bindless and Taylor[6], Lieutenants Erskine, Oland (CANLOAN) and Whitaker, Regimental Sergeant Major Bates and Company Sergeant Majors Jones and King, with a further 26 missing including the also wounded Company Sergeant Major Mowett. Time to reflect was short lived however as another assault would be launched before the month was out – Operation Goodwood.

6 Ken Taylor would go on to play country cricket for Warwickshire after the War.

Men of the 2nd Battalion, Royal Warwickshire Regiment advancing through the wheatfields around Lebisey Wood during Operation Charnwood. 8 July 1944. (Photo: © IWM B6618)

Men of the 2nd Battalion, Royal Warwickshire Regiment advancing through the wheatfields around Lebisey Wood during Operation Charnwood. 8 July 1944. (Photo: © IWM B6619)

Universal Carriers of 2nd Battalion, Royal Warwickshire Regiment pass along a battle scarred lane in the Lebisey area. (Photo: © IWM B6646)

Troops of the Royal Warwickshire Regiment going forward in carriers through a cornfield. (Photo: © IWM B6761)

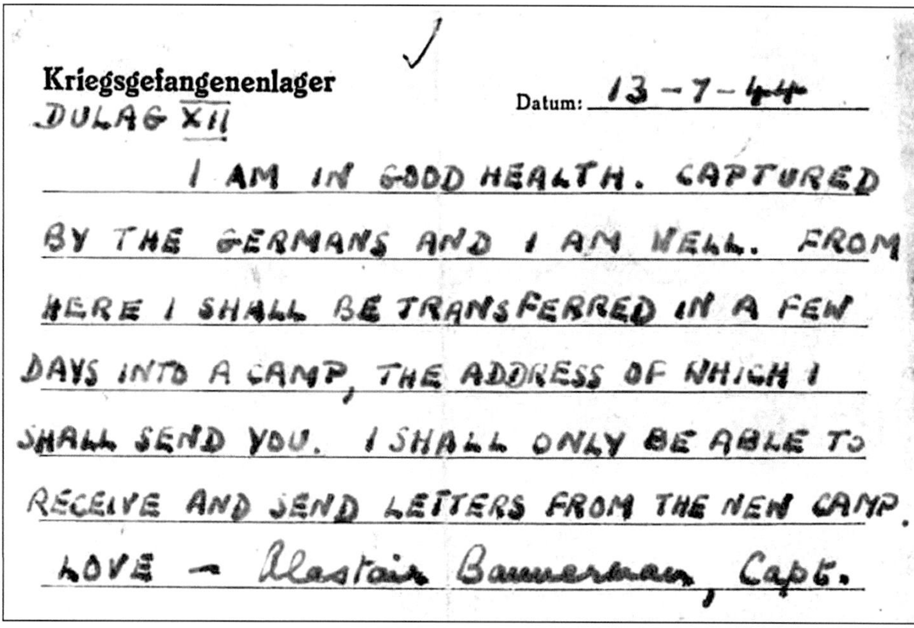

Kriegsgefangenenlager
DULAG XII

Datum: 13-7-44

I AM IN GOOD HEALTH. CAPTURED BY THE GERMANS AND I AM WELL. FROM HERE I SHALL BE TRANSFERRED IN A FEW DAYS INTO A CAMP, THE ADDRESS OF WHICH I SHALL SEND YOU. I SHALL ONLY BE ABLE TO RECEIVE AND SEND LETTERS FROM THE NEW CAMP.

LOVE – Alastair Bannerman, Capt.

Postcard from Captain Alastair Bannerman, sent on 13 July 1944, confirming to his family that he had been taken prisoner. (Photo: Bannerman Family)

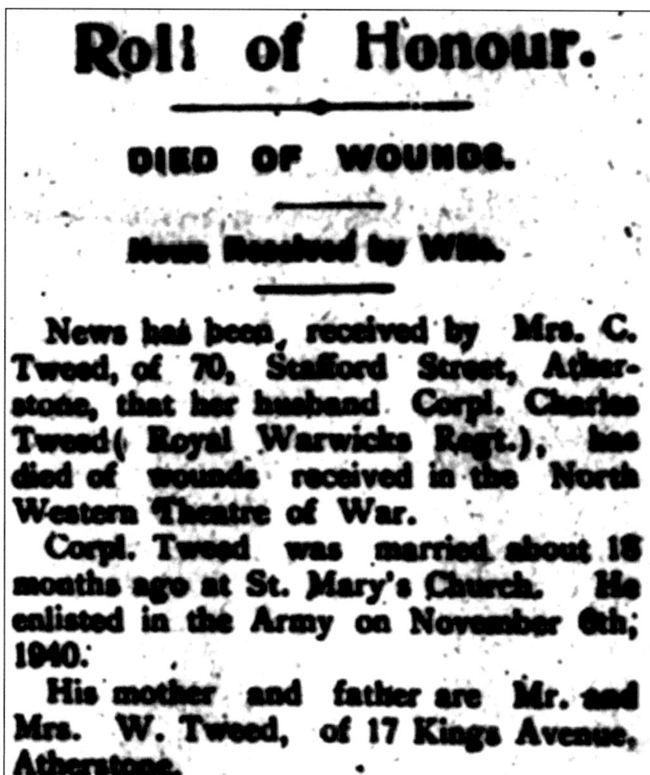

Roll of Honour.

DIED OF WOUNDS.

News Received by Wife.

News has been received by Mrs. C. Tweed, of 70, Stafford Street, Atherstone, that her husband Corpl. Charles Tweed (Royal Warwicks Regt.), has died of wounds received in the North Western Theatre of War.

Corpl. Tweed was married about 18 months ago at St. Mary's Church. He enlisted in the Army on November 6th, 1940.

His mother and father are Mr. and Mrs. W. Tweed, of 17 Kings Avenue, Atherstone.

Roll of honour article in *Atherstone News* dated 4 August 1944. (Photo: Atherstone Library)

Above: Four members of the 2nd Battalion, Royal Warwickshire Regiment, Private Thomas Glen Ruthven Gillespie is second from the right. Date unknown. (Photo: Jason Woods and Royal Warwickshire Regiment Re-enactment Facebook Group)

Left: Temporary grave of Private Thomas Glen Ruthven Gillespie MM, 2nd Battalion, Royal Warwickshire Regiment, who died on 18 July 1944, aged 23. (Photo: Jason Woods and Royal Warwickshire Regiment Re-enactment Facebook Group)

Corporal William John Millard, 2nd Battalion, Royal Warwickshire Regiment, who died on 20 July 1944, aged 23. (Photo: Jason Woods and Royal Warwickshire Regiment Re-enactment Facebook Group)

Private Ernest James Robinson. 2nd Battalion, Royal Warwickshire Regiment, who died on 20 July 1944, aged 19. (Photo: Jason Woods and Royal Warwickshire Regiment Re-enactment Facebook Group)

Private Ronald Sheppard, 2nd Battalion, Royal Warwickshire Regiment, who died on 26 July 1944, aged 23. (Photo: Jason Woods and Royal Warwickshire Regiment Re-enactment Facebook Group)

Private James Arch. 2nd Battalion, Royal Warwickshire Regiment, who died on 2 August 1944, aged 25. (Photo: Jason Woods and Royal Warwickshire Regiment Re-enactment Facebook Group)

Pre-invasion photograph of Private Albert Buckley and Private John Gundy. (Photo: Lindsay Brookes)

Infantrymen of the 2nd Battalion, Royal Warwickshire Regiment carrying mortar shells and moving through wooded country near Le Bény Bocage. 3 August 1944. (Photo: © IWM B8547)

Major Thomas Gordon Bundock DSO MC, D Company, 2nd Battalion, Royal Warwickshire Regiment, killed in action on 6 August 1944, aged 25. (Photo: Royal Regiment of Fusiliers Museum Warwick)

May 1944 photo of Corporal Bill Bowdidge, 18 Platoon, D Coy, 2nd Battalion, Royal Warwickshire Regiment. (Photo: Rob Pettitt)

Private Derrick 'Ginger' Pike and Corporal Bill Bowdidge, D Company, 2nd Battalion, Royal Warwickshire Regiment. January 1944. (Photo: Rob Pettitt)

Above: Captain Peter Batt, speaking about his D-Day experiences in the Rugby School Chapel at a service commemorating the 50th Anniversary of VE Day in 1995. (Photo: Clare Linsell)

Left: Lieutenant D. E. Hosker MC joined 2nd Battalion, Royal Warwickshire Regiment from the 1/7th Batallion when it was disbanded. He was killed in the fighting around Venraij on 19 October 1944. (Photo: Ruud in't Veld)

Sir Dennis Pettitt and his grandchildren, in a photograph taken in the 1990s near the spot at Lebisey where he was wounded for the first time. The edge of the wood can be seen in the background; this is now the edge of a housing development. The field behind them is where he lay wounded until rescued by 'Ginger Pike' and 'Big Robbo'. (Photo: Rob Pettitt)

Private John Gundy, returning to Normandy in 2007 with his granddaughter, to remember his friend Private Albert Buckley for the filming of the excellent documentary, *Finding Buck*. (Photo: courtesy of Lindsay Brookes)

Private Sir Dennis Pettitt, in a photograph taken in Colleville-Montgomery during the commemorations of the 65th D-Day anniversary. (Photo: Rob Pettitt)

Photograph taken in October 1993 in Warwick. Left to right: Captain Clifford Briggs, OC 18 Platoon, D Company; Corporal Bill Bowdidge, 9 Section commander, 18 Platoon, D Company; Doug Robinson, Support Company; Sergeant Reg Moore, 18 Platoon, D Company; Jim Pound, 18 Platoon. Jim Pound transferred to the 2nd Battalion as a reinforcement some time after the battle for Lebisey Wood. (Photo: Rob Pettitt)

Photograph taken June 1994 in Lion-Sur-Mer. Left to right: Company Sergeant Major Russel King, C Company; Ted Bedford, 18 Platoon, D Company; Corporal Bill Bowdidge, D Company. (Rob Pettitt)

The Lebisey Memorial, dedicated to the men of the Royal Warwickshire Regiment. (Photo: Jason Woods)

Final resting place of Corporal Charlie Tweed, C Company, 2nd Battalion, Royal Warwickshire Regiment. Commonwealth War Grave, Douvres, La Delivrande. Plot VIII. Row B. Grave 2. (Photo: Ben Mayne)

8

Goodwood

In the post war period, Operation Goodwood has become notorious as a failed and flawed operation, and while there is no denying the tragedy of heavy losses suffered by the Allies, more recent studies by those more learned than I, demonstrate the purpose that the battle served. Our issue, once again, falls to Monty's personality and his relationship with both colleagues and superiors. Backed by evidence from General Omar Bradley, Commander of 12th US Army Group and General Miles Dempsey CO Second British Army, the aim of Goodwood, and Charnwood before it, was primarily to hold German forces in the Caen area, not necessarily to make a full breakout into the surrounding countryside: 'Go on hitting, drawing the German strength, especially some of the armour, onto yourself – so as to ease the way for Brad.'[1] In this the operation was hugely successful; facing the British and Canadian troops were the vast majority of the SS, Panzer, Infantry and *Fallschirmjäger* divisions available to *Panzergruppe West*. Those not directly facing Second Army would have to be drawn onto them, to prevent them from heading south to face the Americans. The *2.* and *116. Panzerdivisionen* were diverted to the Caen front as a result, opening the door for 12th USAG to eventually launch their own highly successful drive, Operation Cobra. Nobody, however, was opening the door for the British and Canadians, they had to kick it down themselves!

Despite this being the aim, Monty's flippant explanation of the plan, particularly to an exasperated Ike, who Monty did not respect as a field commander, and crucially, his biggest critic, Air Chief Marshal Tedder, left him open to criticism. Tedder, who it can be confidently said loathed Monty, had to be convinced to release Bomber Command from their main purpose of attacking the industrial heartland of the Reich – destroying its ability to wage war. It seems likely that Monty's argument to the RAF: '...setting the whole front aflame...'[2] hinted strongly towards a great breakout from Goodwood, meaning that precious inland airfields would become available to the RAF.

Monty won the argument, but left himself in the impossible position that all others had higher expectations of the operation than would be possible in the face of such a

1 Simon Trew, Simon & Stephen Badsey, *Battle Zone Normandy – Battle or Caen* (Stroud, Sutton Publishing Limited, 2004), p.49
2 Edmund L. Blandford, *Two Sides of the Beach* (Shrewsbury: Airlife Publishing Ltd, 2001), p.201.

strong enemy force. It must be acknowledged that Goodwood was subject to far shorter and less detailed planning than operations that had come before or which would follow later, although there also remains debate as to whether it was Monty or Dempsey who was responsible for the planning. In short, on 18 July British 3rd Infantry Division, now bolstered by 152nd Brigade, would advance through the thickly wooded country from the River Orne in the direction of Emieville and Troarn, and Canadian 2nd & 3rd Infantry Divisions would advance along the front to the south of Caen towards Fleury-sur-Orne and St Martin de Fontenay. Completely misunderstanding the impact of the bocage terrain of Normandy, a massive armoured thrust south-east in the direction of Cagny and Bourgebous, through the industrial heart of Caen on the opposite bank of the River Orne, would be mounted by Guards, 7th and 11th Armoured Divisions – amounting to 1,098 Allied tanks.

With praise lavished on 3rd Division by Dempsey, 2nd Warwicks held their firm base in Lebisey. Straggling groups of German prisoners continued to cross the lines and pass through the battalion, while those Germans still offering resistance subjected the Warwicks to desultory periods of shellfire, which continued to cause injuries; the Battalion IO, Lieutenant P. W. T. Lamb was wounded on 10 July.

On 11 July, 2nd Warwicks moved back and were able to reorganise further at a rest area in Bénouville, where 31 OR specialist reinforcements were received, plus Captain W. S. Cook and Second Lieutenant R. P. Strutt arriving and being posted to C & B Companies respectively. After the hard fighting of the previous weeks, the constant churn of casualties and replacements had taken its toll.

Corporal Alec Graham Pugh
Carrier Platoon, 2nd Battalion, Royal Warwickshire Regiment

> I was tired, a bit jumpy, but elated because we had overcome Lebisey Wood. Which was rather a bogeyman to the battalion, having caught a cold there on D+1.
>
> .... we moved back, I suppose about 5 miles. We were given loads of goodies which the good people of London had collected for us. Air mail, and chocolates and bottles of beer and spirits and all sorts, and suppose the colonel thought it bore us to let us get tiddly and get it out of the system.

Despite the more relaxed environment the battalion found itself in, the enemy was never far away.

Arthur Bullen
2nd Battalion, Royal Warwickshire Regiment

> The place was Normandy in mid-July; a fine sunny day. A football match was in progress. A jazz band entertained. It seemed all very enjoyable if somewhat bizarre! In reality the 2nd Battalion RWR had taken many casualties and was being 'rested' while awaiting reinforcements.
>
> The day passed and darkness was near. It was time to find somewhere to sleep. I found a dry ditch and used my groundsheet and was soon fast asleep. But not for

> long! I was startled by a loud crash and the squealing of terrified horses at a nearby farm. In the distance I heard the bang of a gun and I realised it was coming from somewhere on the coast, almost certainly from Le Havre which was still in enemy hands. The shelling continued for about 20 minutes and fortunately the rounds fell short of my ditch! The firing was erratic and I had a vision of one man making a last act of defiance. All was peaceful again and I pulled the blanket back over my head and resumed my sleep.

Lieutenant Colonel D. L. A. Gibbs DSO
Officer Commanding 2nd Battalion Royal Warwickshire Regiment

> ...we have.... I am afraid, had many changes. We are now a mixture of chaps from various English Counties and from Wales. However, there have been enough 'Royal Warwickshire' flashes to put on their shoulders and they all look the same and are, I think, rapidly being welded together.... The tragedy is that we are not getting good Warwick drafts who are coming over. It's the same old story – we have casualties, we have to be filled up and we get a mixed draft, good chaps but from all over the place. At the same time one hears of a jolly good Warwick draft going off somewhere else. An awful pity.

Baths were made available on 12 July and the battalion was instructed to embark on a period of training, with the promise of at least a week's grace to rest. Plans were hastily drawn up to include junior leaders and sniper cadres. On 13 July Captain A. D. R. Smith, formerly OC Carrier Platoon, became intelligence officer in place of Lieutenant Lamb, and Captain D. R. Fraymouth was appointed C Company second in command. Regimental Quartermaster Sergeant J. Emmett was appointed to take over regimental sergeant major duties. Following Operation Charnwood, Charlie Tweed was promoted to corporal, with the responsibility for his section of 10 men (including himself). Much to the great appreciation of the men, all ranks received their first issue of beer since leaving England, officers were issued with whisky.

As the training schedule began on the morning of 14 July, orders were unceremoniously received for the battalion instead to proceed to Bénouville, taking up position on the eastern bank of the River Orne, where D Company had last been on the night of 6 June, relieving a battalion of 51st Division. Recce parties were promptly dispatched to pave the way for their colleagues. Still technically a reserve position, very little enemy shelling was received and being placed so close to the river, the most troublesome attack came from mosquitos (the insect, not the RAF's de Havilland DH.98!) On 15 July the battalion was officially notified of the awards made from their actions on 7 June; Major Kreyer would receive the Distinguished Service Order, Major Bundock and Captain Illing the Military Cross and Sergeant Pittaway the Military Medal.

By now it was clear that 2nd Warwicks would be involved in another assault. While still in this quiet environment, on the morning of 17 July Brigadier E. Bols held a Brigade O Group to outline each battalion's involvement in the upcoming 2nd Army offensive, to extend the bridgehead across the River Orne to the south and east of Caen. Reminiscent of 6 June, 2nd KSLI would again lead the brigade advance, with the support of the

Sherman tanks of the Staffordshire Yeomanry. 2nd Warwicks would follow up with 1st Norfolks advancing behind, this time the objectives were the villages of Cuillerville and Emieville. After the perceived success of the bombing strategy prior to Operation Charnwood, it was agreed to repeat the process, only this time on a much greater scale.

17 July also spelled the end of Rommel's service on the front line, returning from *1. SS Panzercorps* headquarters, he ignored the warnings against travelling by road in daylight because of the constant threat of Allied fighter aircraft. Approaching the village of Sainte-Foy-de-Montgommery, his car was attacked by Spitfires from 412 Squadron RCAF (602 Squadron RAF are also noted as the possible attackers). The car he was travelling in crashed and Rommel was thrown some distance from the car suffering multiple fractures to the skull. Now gravely wounded, he was once again absent on the eve of an Allied attack.

All 2nd Army artillery batteries commenced the initial bombardment in unison at 0525 hours, targeting pre-sited German anti-aircraft batteries. At 0545 hours, 1,056 RAF Lancaster and Halifax heavy bombers flying in loose formation dropped 3,800 tons of HE on Columbelles, Cagny, Toufreville and Emieville, destroying vast tracts of the built-up area as well as pulverising the positions held by *21. Panzerdivision*. The RAF lost only six aircraft during the raid, but it should be noted that as the anti-aircraft batteries had already been knocked out and in the complete absence of the Luftwaffe, this is not necessarily a comparable statistic.

At 0640 hours, a three-hour long artillery fire plan by the artillery of all three army corps commenced. This, combined with a second wave of bombing from the air wrought utter devastation, there are documented cases of defenders not killed or injured, breaking down under the strain and in some cases even shooting themselves to end the terror.

At 0700 hours 563 tons of fragmentation bombs were dropped on Demouville and Giberville by 318 B-26 Marauders of the US 9th Air Force, shortly after followed by 570 B-24 Liberators dropping another 1,340 tons of fragmentation bombs across the line Troarn – Bourgebus – Frénouville. This was followed up by more than 800 fighter-bombers from RAF 83 and 84 Groups and US 9th Air Force.

Finally, the Royal Artillery's 25-pdrs supporting the armoured thrust began their scheduled rolling barrage at 0745. However, in the confused pall of smoke, fire, dust and debris created by this terrifying bombardment, targets became difficult to identify. Villages like Toufreville in 3rd Division's area of operation were left almost unscathed. While evacuation orders had been imposed by both the Allied and German forces, the greatest tragedy is the civilian loss. More than 3,000 civilians were killed in the combined attacks of Operations Charnwood and Goodwood, only 8,000 buildings were left standing in this once majestic cathedral city and the population had fallen from 60,000 to 17,000.

***Leutnant* Hans Hoeller**

8. Kompanie, 2. Bataillon, Panzergenadierregiment Nr 192

On 18 July 1944, the brief calm was over for us. The British now commenced their decisive attack – Operation Goodwood. It began with a bombardment the likes of which we had never witnessed before. Such was its intensity that those who would survive it would never be able to forget it.... The next thing we heard was the howling of bombs plummeting to the ground before they detonated with a loud crash. Gigantic mushroom clouds rose up and started floating over the terrain ahead. Everyone tried to get as much cover as possible. The air was filled with unbelievable thunder and banging. It seemed as if the world was coming to an end. We had no choice but to endure the entire bombardment in impotent helplessness. Time passed by, but the hellish spectacle continued unabated. All of that, and we were not even in the epicentre of this bombardment. Its main focus lay on a long sector stretching from Colombelles over Cuiverville, up to Toufreville in the north and Cagny in the south.

Impact after impact, the bombardment slowly rolled from north to south. Houses disappeared in flashing explosions, and trees were hurled into the sky. An impenetrable wall of smoke, dust, and detonations formed... It seemed utterly impossible to me that those parts of our *21. Panzerdivision* and *16. Luftwaffe-Feld-Division* that were in this area had any chance of surviving this hell. Such a display of Allied superiority I had never seen before.

Berkeley Meredith
C Squadron, Staffordshire Yeomanry

I've never seen so many planes in my life.... They were going over in a continuous stream out and back. There was a tremendous noise, both from the planes and from the bombardment.

The Guards, 7th and 11th Armoured Divisions began their advance behind the rolling bombardment, the Canadian forces moved forward at 0830 hours with H-Hour for British 3rd Division being led by 152nd Brigade at 0745 hours and 2nd KSLI of 185th Brigade at 0930 hours. 2nd KSLI and the Staffordshire Yeomanry advanced through Lirose but encountering 'stiff fighting' and the loss of much of the armoured support, they came to a halt before the woods of Cuillerville in the early afternoon. The 2nd Warwicks and 1st Norfolks were called up and at 1600 hours ordered to push through the 2nd KSLI as planned and to seize Cuillerville. First however, the battalion had to reach the front line via the narrow corridor created by the initial advance, which was easier said than done.

Private Dennis Pettitt
D Company, 2nd Battalion Royal Warwickshire Regiment

We had a really tough battle at Emieville and Cuillerville. What made it worse was it rained all day, every day for a week. We were slopping about in mud; with the biggest mosquitos I've ever seen. We started out on the start line, with a machine-gun battalion behind us.... Halfway across this turnip field for some reason they opened up behind us.... but then we hit this wall, and we got into the wood at Cuillerville and then we were supposed to have taken Emieville.

One of the most of significant things that happened, was they made me the PIAT gunner, which is what the infantry use against tanks, it's called the projectile infantry anti-tank, The Americans would call it a bazooka. You could fire it from the shoulder, if you'd got any shoulder left, it was heavy and the recoil! BaBumBoom! And you have to wait until the tank is within 70 yards before you can fire effectively. Otherwise it's no good!

Major T. L. Brock
HQ Company, 2nd Battalion Royal Warwickshire Regiment

The attack opened on 18 July according to plan and we spent the morning watching the bombers overhead, and the armour passing through. We were not called up until 4 o'clock in the afternoon, when it was learned that the KSLI had been held up short of the final objective. We moved up to a concentration area and were heavily and accurately shelled on the way.

With A & B Companies leading, along with Battalion HQ, they were subjected to a considerable enemy artillery bombardment and a number of casualties were suffered before they reached Lirose. Lieutenant Colonel Gibbs went ahead to attend an O Group with Brigadier Bols. The proposed plan called for A and C Companies to attack Cuillerville from the west at 2100 hours, with A Company on the right and C Company on the left of the advance. B & D Companies would be held in reserve. At the same time, 7th Field Regiment RA commenced a 30-minute artillery concentration on the objective, some 1,500m ahead of the start line where the leading rifle companies anxiously waited. Most of the battalion troops were now replacements and had not landed on 6 June, but there was still a core of troops who had, and they eyed the ground ahead with trepidation, remembering what they'd witnessed and endured in the recent weeks.

Good progress was made by the initial advance, with the leading companies some 100m short of the woods ahead of Cuillerville, however they were delayed at this point by a high wall blocking their way (reported as 20ft tall in the War Diary, which is almost certainly an exaggeration), and heavy machine gun fire coming down on them and HE shells from a solitary Panzer IV in the nearby woodland. A gap blown earlier in the wall by *Leutnant* Hans Hoeller's *Panzergrenadiers* was eventually found, enabling the two leading companies to continue their advance. However, by now darkness was falling and in the thick undergrowth of the woods they were ordered to halt around 200m short of the town of Cuillerville. The battalion had taken about 40 prisoners, as well as capturing: 'a large amount of equipment including two 88s, and the remains of a 'moaning minnie'.'[3]

Major Robin Kreyer DSO
Second in Command, 2nd Battalion Royal Warwickshire Regiment

We then took part in a big advance to secure a bridgehead south of Caen. The job of the battalion was to advance about 4 miles down a corridor made by the armour and capture a thickly wooded area at the end of it. We put in an attack on this

3 T. L. Brock, 'Account of the battalion in Normandy, Holland & Germany' (Unpublished, date unknown)

> very late in the evening and in spite of awful confusion in the dark in the woods managed to get a secure position for the night which was improved by a further advance early next morning. The Bn took a lot of prisoners and some guns and tanks in this attack without many casualties at this stage – due to the tremendous battering our air force had given the Boche.... I got wounded the second day of all this so I was lucky enough to miss the worst of it.

One of the many tragedies of the battle was the loss of the battalion's youngest member. Seventeen years old, Private Alan Roberts,[4] from Small Heath, Birmingham, had lied about his age on his enlistment papers and was sadly killed during the attack on Cuillerville Woods.

At dawn the next day the advance continued with Brigade RA laying on a fresh artillery programme. However, an error had been made in the positioning of the forward companies, and a number of casualties were suffered with 'friendly' fire falling on their positions. With 1st Norfolks on the left, A and C Companies formed a solid front line through which a much depleted B and D Companies could advance and dig in around Cuillerville. D Company had the added support of Lieutenant J. Martin-Webb's platoon from C Company, whereas B Company had suffered the loss of most of its Company HQ from enemy shelling, with only Major G. E. E. Ross remaining uninjured.

In that ingrained Prussian tradition, the German troops counter-attacked. At 1800 hours *125. Panzergrenadiers* with the support of two Panzer VI Tigers took the battalion by surprise. Major Ross himself was wounded by mortar fire and B Company was forced to retire under the weight of the attack. Their withdrawal was assisted by the heroic actions of 23-year-old Corporal William John Millard, of Darlaston. With heavy MG-42 fire coming from the direction of Emieville, just ahead of their position, Corporal Millard taking his Bren Gun, rushed forward firing from the hip, taking out an enemy position and killing two of their number, but he was mortally wounded before he could retire with the rest of B Company. As part of the BEF, Jack (William John) Millard, had served in France in 1940 with the 2nd Battalion, surviving the fighting retreat to the coast and finally being evacuated from Dunkirk on 30 May 1941.

Major Bundock's D Company, plus Lieutenant Martin-Webb's Platoon gallantly held their ground. Ever leading by example, Major Bundock came forward asking Private Dennis 'Nifty' Pettitt for instruction on the PIAT he carried. Major Bundock then armed himself with the weapon and took it upon himself to turn the tide. Stalking forward alone towards one of the Tigers, he took aim and miraculously (his first time using this notoriously inaccurate weapon) struck and disabled the tank. With the German crew hastily exiting the burning hulk, he quietly returned to his men placing the weapon back into the care of Private Pettitt. For his gallantry in this action, Major Bundock MC was deservedly recommended for the DSO.

4 Private Alan Roberts is listed as being 19 years old on his gravestone in Ranville War Cemetery.

Private Dennis Pettitt
D Company, 2nd Battalion Royal Warwickshire Regiment

> … and then we got attacked by tanks, and me and a bloke called Deakin…. were in the same slit trench on the edge of this great bomb crater that had been caused by us of course, the RAF had bombed the hell out of it…
>
> And then coming towards us were these tanks, and what they called panzer grenadiers. And all these grenadiers, dozens of them, are coming firing at us. And Tom Bundock says, "Who's got the PIAT gun?" I said, "Me Sir!" He said, "Right give it me!" Within about 50 yards, he's lying on this little wall, I said, "You'd better fire quick Sir…" I'm sure more by luck than judgement he hit this tank, it shuddered to a halt, spun round like this. And the other tank, there were two tanks…. they thought with two Tigers bearing down on us we'd do a bunk, but we didn't of course, because we'd knocked the tank out. So they turned and ran.

Returning to my original focus, on 19 July 1944, Corporal Charlie Tweed died of wounds received during the advance. Alas, in the much regretted absence of his service records, no details are available as to the exact cause of his death or the date on which he received his wounds. It is possible that he was fatally wounded as part of the platoon from C Company led by Lieutenant Martin-Webb, supporting Major Bundock's D Company holding against the German counter-attack. Most of the fallen from 2nd Warwicks during Goodwood are buried in Ranville Commonwealth War Grave; as Charlie is buried some distance away, in Douvres La Délivrande, it is likely he was wounded during the Goodwood advance, or even prior to the attack, and was transported back via the field dressing station at Hermanville, and/or the casualty clearing station on the outskirts of Douvres, before succumbing to his wounds. He was buried in the temporary cemetery at La Délivrande before being moved to his final CWGC plot. His headstone reads:

> WE WILL ALWAYS REMEMBER YOU WHEN THE REST OF THE WORLD FORGETS

Unknown to the men of 185th Brigade, the enemy troops ahead of them began to slowly withdraw during the night of 19/20 July under cover of heavy artillery shelling that would continue sporadically for the coming days. On 20 July, D Company was able to withdraw from their defensive positions with C Company taking their place in the line, Private Ernest James Robinson of Selly Park, Birmingham was killed on this day. As C Company explored the ground they now occupied, they discovered many enemy panzers disabled or destroyed by the incredible bombardment that preceded the attack on 18 July, some having been turned over entirely onto their turret by the force of the blasts.

Corporal Alec Graham Pugh
Carrier Platoon, 2nd Battalion, Royal Warwickshire Regiment

> … just outside Troarn, quite a severe battle took place in wooded country. And we finished up in a salient and was subjected to days of intense mortar and artillery fire from all sides by German armed forces…. during this it was raining and dark and when we dug in we were that close we could hear the Germans talking…
>
> …under a particularly heavy bombardment one day, the shells hit the slit trench in which I was in and as result I was evacuated to the first aid post and then the military hospital, just scattered shrapnel, very small slivers of shrapnel in the shoulder, as well as being frightened to death!

Although the Allied troops on the ground did not know, momentous events were taking place elsewhere. On 20 July, an assassination attempt was made on Hitler's life in a failed attempt to overthrow the Nazi regime. *Oberst* Claus Schenk Graf von Stauffenberg had placed a briefcase containing a bomb beneath the table at which Hitler and leading figures were meeting in the *Wolfsschanze*. Although wounded in the explosion, Hitler survived.

With Operation Goodwood over and under continued fire from enemy artillery, a patrol was sent forward on the 21st towards Emieville, which had been the battalion's ultimate Goodwood objective. Finding it now unoccupied, the battalion held position so that the 2nd KSLI could come forward in greater strength to consolidate the newly captured town.

Major Robin Kreyer DSO
Second in Command, 2nd Battalion Royal Warwickshire Regiment

> We then had to hold this position for six very unpleasant days under very heavy shell fire and several counter-attacks by Infantry and Tanks.
>
> D Company under Tom Bundock did wonderful work during this period and Tom himself, drove off a Tiger Tank with a P.I.A.T. Our casualties were pretty heavy during this period – we were very sorry to lose our doctor…. who was killed, he had done magnificently throughout. Our new IO…. who came from Worcesters – was also killed and Mike Ryan, A Company Commander was badly wounded. The new R.S.M. Emmett who had been R.Q.M.S. was also wounded.

On 22 July, Battalion HQ commandeered the cellar of a nearby Chateau in Emieville, while the other companies remained in foxholes and improvised dug outs. Heavy enemy shelling continued and on the 23rd Captain Alfred Smith, Bn IO was killed. On 24 July the battalion was finally taken out of the line, being replaced by 10th Battalion Durham Light Infantry of 43rd Infantry Division. Brigade motor transport provided the means for it to relocate to a rest area near Mathieu (listed as Cazelle in the Battalion War Diary).

Post battle the battalion was now able to take stock and reassess its strength. In addition, five other officers were wounded: Major R. G. Kreyer, Major G. E. E. Ross, Major M. Ryan, Captain J. H. T. Lawton and Second Lieutenant T. L. Williams. Fortunately,

Major Kreyer was able to return to the battalion on 27 July, but Major Ryan had taken quite a serious head wound, and sadly John Lawton of the RAMC died of the wounds he had received on 1 August 1944. Another two officers, Captain R. W. Heath and Lieutenant C. B. Bubb, after such trying ordeals understandably required a period of recuperation through battle exhaustion. Captain Heath had been in the line continually since landing on 6 June. Regimental Sergeant Major J. Emmett, and Company Sergeant Majors Launchbury and Mills were also wounded. Of the sadly unnamed other ranks, 34 were killed and 202 wounded, with 12 listed as missing – amongst the 34 were Private Arthur 'Dusty' Miller of Warwick, Private Thomas Gillespie of Kirkaldy, Fife, and Corporal Charles Tweed.

Lieutenant Colonel D. L. A. Gibbs DSO
Officer Commanding, 2nd Battalion Royal Warwickshire Regiment

> In spite of more losses everyone is in very good heart, and we are of course all much braced up by the goings on the American front. This is very encouraging to us all who have been bearing the brunt of things – in pretty fierce, unpleasant and costly conditions. Mike Ryan has been wounded as has also (rather badly I am afraid) our very delightful doctor. Captain D. Smith (not Warwicks) has been killed, he was a delightful chap and did so well.

With so many officers now out of action, even temporarily, a considerable reorganisation was necessary. Major T. L. Brock became acting battalion second in command, Lieutenants Clarke, Aylward and Cook were promoted acting captain and Captain Barratt despite nearly losing his watch earlier in the campaign, now became acting major. Company Sergeant Major Lewis, who arrived with 11 other replacements, took on the duties of regimental sergeant major.

Despite disappointment at Supreme Headquarters Allied Expeditionary Force, and in the home and US press, Monty saw Goodwood as largely successful. 3rd Division had reached almost all objectives, not quite reaching Troarn, and the armoured thrust, expected by some to advance on Falaise, had been halted after only 8km. If, as he maintained, the purpose was to spare the US Forces further south the depredations of facing more armoured divisions, then we can support this, there were however still heavy losses during Goodwood, and not just to the combatants. Militarily, 493 tanks were damaged, and of these 156 were permanently out of action and there were over 5,500 casualties. From the civilian perspective, and not just in Caen, it was far far worse, in addition to around 15,000 French civilians killed in Normandy by Allied bombing raids in the build-up to the invasion, another 19,890 were killed during the Battle for Normandy. 120,000 buildings were completely destroyed with another 270,000 seriously damaged, 116,000sq ft of factory space was damaged and 118,000 acres of farmland were left unusable. We cannot underestimate the impact this had on those that had been liberated.

Private Dennis Pettitt
D Company, 2nd Battalion Royal Warwickshire Regiment

> And then we went for a day's rest where you could have a shower, change your socks, go to the loo without being shot at. It was a very tiny village, the mayor didn't like us one bit, because he had a little smallholding and of course, most of our people had been in the front line without proper food, and they started to dig up his vegetables and tomatoes. So next morning, a parade was called. (Lieutenant Colonel Gibbs said) the mayor has told me, that in four years, the Bosch never touched anything, one day and British have taken everything.

Now behind the lines, things looked very different, but the tragic aftereffects of Goodwood still followed them. On 26 July, while all ranks were able to visit the divisional club and corps rest camp, Private Ronald Sheppard of Stourbridge lost his life and is now buried in Bayeux. The mobile bath units were available and some of the men were able to visit the cinema. Monty, accompanied by Major General Whistler, the divisional commander visited the battalion on 27 July, having presented the various divisional awards at Brigade HQ. In his usual style, Monty paid visits to the men in each company, ensuring he was seen as well as heard before heading to the Officers' Mess for tea. A large proportion of the ORs were also able to see George Formby entertaining the troops at a corps rest camp.

Word arrived on 28 July that the battalion would have a few days' rest and once more training programmes and cadres were compiled, only to have these dashed again. Orders were received the following day to return east of the Orne River to relieve a 9th Brigade battalion in the line, and that afternoon recce parties went forward to meet them while the men prepared themselves and got their kit together to move. The ever frustrating changes of plan continued to hamper them, first the move was postponed for 24 hours, then on 31 July, much to the delight of all, the move was cancelled altogether and 3rd Division became GHQ Reserve. During this time, a healthy sized replacement draft arrived including the then Company Sergeant Major William Lewis, and from 2nd Battalion Hertfordshire Regiment, Lieutenant C. W. Moxham and 33 ORs that were posted to D Company, while A Company received Lieutenant F. A. E. Bonney MC, Private Walter Charles Gray and 33 other ORs. Lieutenant Bonney and Private Gray had landed on Gold Beach with the 2nd Herts on 6 June. Lieutenant Bonney was awarded the MC for his actions that day, his citation read:

> On June 6 1944, Lieut. Bonney found that three of his men had been left on a road which was under heavy enemy fire. Taking a Bren Gun and a corporal with him, he crawled back under MG and mortar fire to rescue these men. On reaching them, he found that two had been killed and one wounded. Assisted by his corporal, Lieut. Bonney brought back the wounded man at great personal risk.

Wally Gray had been 14 at the outbreak of the war, he joined the local Home Guard at 16 and at 18 enlisted into the Hertfordshire Regiment. 'His' battalion was later broken up during the Normandy campaign and the men distributed as required; given the option of returning to the UK or remaining with his mates and joining another battalion in the line, Private Gray chose the latter.

Lieutenant Colonel D. L. A. Gibbs DSO
Officer Commanding 2nd Battalion Royal Warwickshire Regiment

During a few days' rest we have managed to freshen and smarten ourselves up a lot and, with it, there has been a lot of good entertainment for the troops. We have also managed to hold an inter-coy football knockout competition which HQ Coy won.

I have had two RSMs in about a fortnight! Bates, wounded and at home somewhere and his successor also wounded. I have now got a CSM Lewis.... He has done about 18 years with 1st Bn. Monty came to see us the other day and was in the greatest form. There were several here who knew him and whom he knew, and he spoke to all the chaps from a jeep, which they loved, and then had tea with the officers. Altogether a great success.

Major Robin Kreyer DSO
Second in Command, 2nd Battalion Royal Warwickshire Regiment

The Bn is full of new faces since 'D' Day but newcomers have become R. Warwickshires very quickly and the Bn is in great heart. Colonel Gibbs is a magnificent CO and everyone is very happy. General Montgomery came and had tea with the Bn a few days ago and talked to everyone who had known him.

Major T. L. Brock
HQ Company, 2nd Battalion Royal Warwickshire Regiment

Cazelle (Mathieu) proved to be a very pleasant village, well way from the sounds of battle. There we received a good batch of reinforcements, including CSM Lewis, who was appointed RSM in place of Regimental Sergeant Major J. Emett, who had been wounded at Emieville. By this time various schemes for rest and entertainment had got into their stride and we were able to get quite a large proportion of the battalion away to the divisional club and the corps rest camp. The cinema and ENSA were also available.

Neither was training neglected, although facilities were somewhat limited, range work and route marches were carried out. Our football kit was unpacked and the inter-company knockout competition was won by HQ Company, who defeated B Company in the final. On 31 July our division left 1st Corps and became GHQ Reserve.

9

Breakout

Following Goodwood, considerable forces were reallocated by *OKW*. Bolstering the forces facing the British and Canadian troops were now *2. SS Panzerdivision 'Das Reich'*, *9. SS Panzerdivision 'Hohenstaufen'*, *12. SS Panzerdivision 'Hitlerjugend'* and elements of *10. SS Panzerdivision 'Frundsberg'*, as well as the *Panzer-Lehr-Division*, forces which would have otherwise been free to hamper the US advance on St Lo. The focus of the Anglo-Canadian Divisions now was to hold the Caen front, while wheeling in a south-easterly direction as the US force advanced north, ultimately creating the Falaise Pocket in an attempt to capture the bulk of the retreating German Army Group B.

At the start of August, as a small cog in the Operation Bluecoat machine, the battalion was instructed to move forward north of Caumont to a concentration area, spending the night of 2 August in an orchard. On 3 August 185th Brigade, including 2nd Warwicks, came under the temporary command of 29th Armoured Brigade, 11th Armoured Division. The 11th Armoured Division advance had temporarily halted, and infantry reinforcement was urgently needed. The battalion was therefore to move to the Le Bény Bocage region, fortunately their legs were saved and the RASC provided 20 three-ton lorries to transport the men via Anguerny, Secqueville-en-Bessin and Coulombs. After a number of warm dry days, the roads were thick with dust, raising great clouds into the sky as they motored along. Fortunately, despite the 'Dust Means Death' signs, the movement went unnoticed by the enemy.

The level of detail captured within the War Diaries and Operational Orders of the time, produced and signed by Captain Peter Batt as adjutant, are fascinating in their minutiae. Each man would carry two days' rations, speed was limited to 15mph, halts were ordered for 10 minutes upon each even numbered hour on the clock, only side lights and under carriage lights would be used on the lorries and the leading vehicle would carry a blue light and flag, and the rearmost vehicle green (the practice of these coloured flags is still continued today).

Major T. L. Brock
HQ Company, 2nd Battalion Royal Warwickshire Regiment

It was with great difficulty that we were able to complete the necessary preparations by nightfall. This was our first experience of the difficult 'bocage' country, with its dusty tracks, all ranks suffered considerably from the dust and sun.

That afternoon, they moved forward and came under orders to retake Presles and re-establish contact with forward elements of 29th Armoured Brigade. The village had fallen to an enemy counter-attack and now lay threateningly between 23rd Hussars and the Motor Battalion of 8th Rifle Brigade and their Brigade HQ. A night attack was planned and at midnight the battalion advanced, D Company taking the left of the advance and C Company the right; armour and artillery support was provided by 29th Armoured Brigade. A and B Companies operated in a support role, following close behind.

Private Dennis Pettitt
D Company, 2nd Battalion Royal Warwickshire Regiment

We started from La Beny Bocage, towards Presles and we took that without a shot being fired. After, when we took Presles, we were sent out on patrol to make contact with the 11th Armoured Division. Because they'd been cut off by the Germans, so we had to go and rescue them. Don't we always in the infantry!

As they advanced towards Presles, the battalion crossed the north easterly road from Vire to Estry, ironically codenamed WARWICK by 11th Armoured Division, the modern D55. As it was, the advance was peaceful as the enemy had already withdrawn in the face of the advancing forces. However, remaining in a location recently vacated by German troops was not advisable, a known and effective German tactic was to pre-register their positions as artillery targets for this very eventuality. So, after a peaceful morning the village was comprehensively bombarded by German artillery.

Major T. L. Brock
HQ Company, 2nd Battalion Royal Warwickshire Regiment

The next morning was quiet, and nothing happened until mid-day, when suddenly a salvo of *nebelwerfers* landed in the village, killing RSM Lewis and causing several other casualties. Shelling then continued at intervals throughout the day. In all probability the lack of activity during the morning had caused us to think that we were not under observation; always an unwise thought!

At 1300 hours, divisional orders were issued for 2nd Warwicks to relieve 8th Rifle Brigade near Le Bas Perrier, who would take up position themselves in Presles. The order stated that this should be completed by 1800 hours, but with limited time available and continued enemy fire, this was far more challenging than it seemed to those at Divisional HQ. However, the battalion pushed on, and despite taking heavy casualties from enemy shelling on the march, they successfully relieved 8th Rifle Brigade by 2000 hours.

The battalion took up position just short of the village of Le Bas Perrier. Its defences were bolstered by 23rd Hussars, along with a troop of SPs and a troop of AVREs. With the added support, 'This force was very thick on the ground,'[1] As such, it was agreed that Captain Field's B Company the following day would advance a few hundred metres into Le Bas Perrier itself and take up position in the lower ground in the surrounding houses and orchards where they would take and hold the position. This manoeuvre was carried out successfully on 5 August, one platoon however advanced further than intended. The enemy, noticing the platoon out on a limb, exploited the opportunity and counter-attacked. C Company was sent forward to support B Company who were taking casualties. After the counter-attack dispersed, both B and C Companies remained in Le Bas Perrier, which was overlooked by a nearby ridge, while the understrength A and D Companies held the original position on higher ground with the armour. A monument to 11th Armoured Division now stands in Le Bas Perrier.

While the overlooking high ground posed an issue to the defenders now in the village, it also represented a significant boon to the brigade. If it could be taken and held it would offer a vital observation point on the other side of the ridge towards Chenedolle, the brigade's next objective. Unknown to the Allies, the German defenders had bolstered their own lines and they prepared to launch a counter-attack on 6 August, the same day that B Company were instructed to proceed to the ridge line and establish a standing patrol on its crest. They advanced through the scrub unopposed, but upon taking the ridge were met by advancing troops of *9. SS Panzerdivision 'Hohenstaufen'*, who were in the process of taking the ridge themselves. The ridge was fiercely contested by both sides, close hand-to-hand fighting ensued as each man was lost in his own battle with the man in front of him. Eventually, B Company was forced to withdraw under the weight of the SS attack, returning to their original position in Le Bas Perrier. B Company suffered some 30 casualties, of which 18 were missing.

Major T. L. Brock
HQ Company, 2nd Battalion Royal Warwickshire Regiment

> On 5 August Cpl E. Browne displayed exceptional courage in taking on a lone MG post at LE BAS PERRIER, together with Pte C Harris, also of D Company, without thought for their own safety, he charged straight at the post firing his Bren Gun. He succeeded in knocking out the crew and capturing the gun. For this action he was awarded the Military Medal.
>
> Other men who were noticeable for their bravery were Pte J O'Halloran, 'D' Company, Pte J Parkes, the CO's bodyguard, who was a tower of strength, and three men of the Mortar Platoon, Pte E Clarke, Pte G Hooper and Pte A Welch. These latter three continued to serve their mortars with ammunition under intense artillery fire, thus enabling them to remain in action at a critical moment.

1 TNA WO 171/1387, '2nd Battalion, the Royal Warwickshire Regiment, War Diary,' 4 August 1944.

While C Company fought on the ridge, the rest of the battalion were under heavy artillery fire and taking casualties of their own. The area around A and D Companies with the armoured support took a heavy pounding, causing at least one of the Shermans to 'brew up'. In an act of the utmost bravery, Major Bundock ran forward to rescue the crew of a burning tank, which was positioned near to one of his sections. In defiance of this gallantry, the tank exploded as he climbed on board, killing him instantly along with the wounded crew. Tom Bundock, dashing and brave, was a greatly respected and much-liked officer, the men under his command had complete confidence in him as a soldier and leader. His loss was a devastating blow to both the battalion, and to his wife Fiona, who had already lost her brother Hugh in Normandy.[2]

Private Ted Bedford
D Company, 2nd Battalion Royal Warwickshire Regiment

> In August the battalion was involved in heavy fighting during which a supporting tank was hit just a few yards from D Company personnel.
>
> Major Bundock climbed on to the tank to check for survivors. He ascertained no one was alive and started to throw out ammunition, being concerned for the safety of D Company. Unfortunately, the tank received another hit and Major Bundock was killed. He was an officer greatly respected by all ranks and he was sorely missed.

A concentration of enemy infantry and armour was identified moving along the ridgeline around 1600 hours, while a heavy barrage from both artillery and mortars began to rain down on the battalion's position. Gibbs immediately requested defensive fire from 27th Field Regiment RA and Brigade artillery, to strike along the skyline, but the German attack was not deterred. SS troops made contact along the line, in too close for artillery support to take effect, and a small force of infantry and two Panzer IVs penetrated B Company lines, in the ensuing mayhem inflicting a number of casualties. B Company rifle fire was no match, and the men were forced to find cover as tank tracks ground the earth about their positions.

While B Company appeared to be in disarray, C Company resolutely held their position, allowing B Company to form a new defensive line and enabling the 23rd Hussars to engage the SS Panzer IV's. The new line held; the SS direct attack would not reach Le Bas Perrier, so they reformed into two flanking positions, attempting to encircle 2nd Warwicks in the little hamlet. For some four hours, 2nd Warwicks and 23rd Hussars were engaged, with artillery from both sides adding to the havoc. As dusk set in, the German forces began to retreat. The ingrained discipline of the battalion's men, coupled with the support and supplies available took their toll, and no matter how hard they pushed, the SS could not break the defences. It was a hard won engagement, and the price had been high for both sides, a number of German soldiers had been captured and were taken for interrogation.

2 Lieutenant Colonel Hugh Herdon, commanding officer 2nd Battalion the Royal Warwickshire Regiment

Despite this victory, there was no let up. Throughout the 7th, the battalion was heavily bombarded by well-directed machine-gun, anti-tank and artillery fire. One of the Panzer IV's from the previous day's assault had survived and continued to cause C Company difficulties until it was eventually halted by a patrol, fighting their way forward and disabling it. They held position, but once more, casualties had been heavy, and the Hussars had lost a number of their Shermans to direct anti-tank gun fire.

Major T. L. Brock
HQ Company, 2nd Battalion Royal Warwickshire Regiment

> The… day was marked by attempts by Bosche SP Guns to get into positions where they could dominate the battalion area. In this they achieved some success, but were eventually forced to withdraw.

A battalion of the Herefordshire Regiment had been ordered to relieve the Warwicks on 8 August. Once these orders had been received the battalion put forth a small reconnaissance patrol during the morning, to ensure the smooth running of the day and ensure against an enemy attack. However, the Germans endeavoured to make their presence known and throughout the evening shelled their position, meaning the exchange of positions was a brief affair, with the men of the Herefords unimpressed at their new surroundings.

2nd Warwicks fell back to Presles by 0300 hours on 9 August, taking over the position previously held by the unhappy Herefords. The fighting of the last 6 days during Operation Bluecoat had seen a number of casualties suffered. In addition to Major Bundock, 22 ORs had been killed. Captain Peter Batt (adjutant), Captain D. A. Field (OC B Company), Captain Cook (Mortar Plat.), Captain Clarke (Second in Command B Company), Lieutenants Bonney (Platoon Commander A Company) and Groom (intelligence officer), plus 143 ORs were wounded, with a further 30 ORs reported missing.

Captain Peter Batt
Adjutant, 2nd Battalion Royal Warwickshire Regiment

> I'll move on…. to the day I was wounded. By then the regiment had lost about 35 officers, that's 100 percent in numbers, and about 350 men, that's half. And so my turn had really come.
>
> …fifty years on, I went to a regimental reunion at Warwick, and a man came up to me and said. "Do you remember me Sir?" And of course I didn't. He said, "I was one end of the stretcher when you were wounded." And he went on to recount the moment in detail, I remembered it too. How they were carrying me across a field, an almighty stonk…. took place and it was very heavy, thinking of their own safety, and who can blame them, they dropped the stretcher and ran for their lives into the ditches and when the stonk was over they knew that I was dead, but they thought they'd better pick their stretcher up in case they got some more casualties, but they found that I was alive.

A short visit to a divisional rest area five miles south of Le Bény Bocage was possible on 9 August. Once more, motor transport was on hand to transfer the battalion, with it finally arriving at 1600 hours. Happily, the evening brought the welcome news they would be re-joining 3rd Division. This also brought new orders, that the following day they would be heading to a forward concentration area, in readiness for the pending advance upon Tinchebray, scene of a battle in 1106 between Henry I of England and the Duke of Normandy. With so little time available it was imperative that the battalion organise itself. With so many casualties and no realistic hope of replacements, 2nd Warwicks reformed with just three rifle companies (A, C and D). Major Jerram, the only remaining S Company officer, was brother to Lieutenant Colonel Jerram, CO 1/7th Warwicks.

Re-allocation of Battalion Officers – 9 August 1944

Battalion HQ	Lieutenant Colonel D. L. A. Gibbs DSO – OC Major T. L. Brock – 2IC Lieutenant A. R. Allen – Acting Adjutant Lieutenant F. J. Groom – Acting IO	
A Company	Captain M. L. B. Hall – OC	
Platoon Commanders	Lieutenant O. W. Jarvis	2nd Lieutenant R. P. Strutt
C Company	Major W. T. Barratt – OC	
Platoon Commanders	Lieutenant J. Martin-Webb	Lieutenant D. S. B. Roberts
D Company	Captain F. Bell MM – OC	
Platoon Commanders	Lieutenant J. S. Clarke	Lieutenant C. W. Moxham
Support Company	Major C. F. J. Jerram – OC	

As the Falaise Pocket began to form, German forces increased the speed of their retreat, but this was not a rabble making a break for it. The retreat was steady, holding up the advancing Allies and leaving behind the ubiquitous mix of snipers, minefields and booby traps expected of German troops.

Corporal Bill Bowdidge
9 Section Commander, 18 Platoon, D Company, 2nd Battalion, Royal Warwickshire Regiment

> …on 10 Aug I rejoined the Bn & was shocked to find Tom had been killed & there were so few of the old D Coy left including some who like me had returned after wounds in the first battle at Lebisey. There were not enough to form one section without including three or four new reinforcements. I was the only original corporal, so my section was formed of four or five original D Coy men plus the reinforcements.
>
> We immediately set off to go forward & on one occasion my section was the point section of the Bn in a linear advance. We eventually dug in in our forward

> position & during the next couple of days led my section on recce patrols & a night listening patrol, during which we were repeatedly shelled by our own 25 pounders!

With motor transport unavailable, the men took to their feet. The battalion marched to the forward concentration area, which was some three miles to the east of Vire, just north of the railway. They were permitted a quiet night's rest, for they were to be woken the following morning by a pre-registered bombing programme ahead of 0900 hours, when 185th Brigade and 8th Brigade would commence their advance. 8th Brigade's objective was Point 272 to the right of the main Vire – Tinchebray road. The objective of 185th Brigade was Point 312, around 2km east of La Maslerie, between Roullours and Creully. 2nd KSLI would lead the advance with 2nd Warwicks following. 1st Norfolks, now reduced to just two companies, was the reserve battalion bringing up the rear.

As ever, things changed. As dawn broke there was a thick ground mist all around and the artillery bombardment was cancelled, however by 0900 hours the mist had cleared and a clear sky and a bright sun reigned over the battlefield, recreating the stifling heat of the first days after their landing in June. Regardless of the missing artillery support, the advance began on time. Vire was cleared, and 2nd KSLI advanced through Roullours, probing slowing forward towards Point 312, all movement was hindered by mines.

Positioned in the orchards one mile to the north of Roullours, at 1200 hours, the Warwicks themselves moved out, clearing Roullours behind the 2nd KSLI. They continued through the thick maze-like bocage country towards La Maslerie. At around 1700 hours the battalion reached La Maslerie, immediately having to dig in, as artillery fire fell on them from the retreating defenders. As dusk fell, having cleared the surrounding area, particularly the orchard, where A Company took a number of casualties, the battalion formed a strong position at La Maslerie, where they remained for the night. 2nd KSLI had taken up position upon Point 312, with 1st Norfolks remaining in Roullours.

The advance continued the following morning at 0800 hours with 2nd Warwicks leading. D Company, now led by Captain Bell MM, led unopposed, reaching a crossroads just to the north of Creully. However, with Major Barratt's C Company following up, they came under mortar fire, and taking cover from the barrage, found themselves surrounded by mines and booby traps, with a number of men killed or wounded in both companies. The battalion was ordered to take up position on the crossroads. A number of patrols were sent out some 2,000m to the south-east, along a small stream to the south of Creully. The other battalions moved up in line with the Warwicks' position, meaning no further advance was required on 12 August.

Intelligence reports suggested the *3. Fallschirmjägerdivision*, then under command of *Generalleutnant* Richard Schimpf, was forming a rearguard in Creully. On 13 August, a number of patrols were sent out to confirm this and to identify the enemy positions. A C Company platoon, led by Lieutenant Martin-Webb, made direct contact and a small firefight ensued, with Lieutenant Martin-Webb and two of his men wounded. C Company took up forward positions but were periodically shelled throughout the day. That evening, the battalion was ordered to put in an attack on this force of airborne troops in Creully. At 2000 hours, D & C Companies advanced, D to the left and C the right.

Major T. L. Brock
HQ Company, 2nd Battalion Royal Warwickshire Regiment

On the evening of 13 August Maj Bell MM was commanding D Company in an attack on LE BOIS. As already described the enemy artillery and mortar fire was very heavy and lasted throughout most of the 1,000 yards advance to the objective. The result was that D Company suffered a high percentage of casualties and by the time the objective was gained could only muster 20 men. Maj Bell's leadership under the most difficult conditions was of the highest order and there is no doubt that it was almost entirely due to him the Company gained its objective.

In this action Maj Bell was most ably supported by Captain O. W. Moxham who commanded his platoon in a most gallant fashion.

Cpl V. Garrett, D Company, commanded the leading section in this attack, he led his men quite fearlessly until the objective was gained. He then found that he had only one man left beside himself. In spite of this he searched the objective for Germans and whenever he found any, promptly dispatched them. For this action he was subsequently awarded the Military Medal.

Corporal Bill Bowdidge
9 Section Commander, 18 Platoon, D Company, 2nd Battalion, Royal Warwickshire Regiment

I wrote a letter to my parents on the 13th which they kept & I still have. In the afternoon Major Bell had a briefing for officers & NCOs in which we were told our orders were to advance 1,000 yards, no opposition expected, start time 2000. We climbed out of our trenches & immediately all hell was let loose, big guns, medium guns & machine guns were firing in both directions. Soon the troops ahead of us were halted, my section had reached a farm yard.

Two troops of Churchill tanks of the 4th Battalion Coldstream Guards supported each company. As the two already understrength companies formed up, Major Barratt, OC C Company was wounded[3], Major Brock, Battalion Second in Command, was rushed forward to command C Company for the attack. As soon as the advance began, both companies were subjected to heavy shell and mortar fire, and a further large number of casualties was incurred.[4] Against the incoming fire, C Company was unable to advance any further, however D Company reported that they had reached its objective.

Private Walter Charles Gray
D Company, 2nd Battalion Royal Warwickshire Regiment

... we were attacking a farmhouse.... it was on a corner.... it was all little lanes with very high hedges, and there was a hill going up, and when we got there I was told to go with another man, and go round the side of the bunker, this farm-house. So we went round the side and there was a slope behind us and when they

3 Major Barratt was the last remaining company commander from the 6 June landings.
4 Around 70 percent of Allied casualties in Normandy were attributed to mortar fire.

attacked the farm house, they attacked it with something called a PIAT. Now the PIAT, it fired a rocket.... the rocket banged into the front of this building, and there was a big flash of flames.... well they used it on this farmhouse.... we were around the side, suddenly there was a big burst of flames against the windows and all that, and the Germans started running out the back, I was with this other chap, so we started firing at them, and then a machine gun started firing at us.... and the bullets were kind of very low.... you could see them hitting the ground, they were just within range, I got hit in the neck and a bullet went in this leg (points to his right leg), and the man I was with.... it went into his back, when that happened we just decided to go back from where we came from, because we were both walking okay.

Private Dennis Pettitt
D Company, 2nd Battalion Royal Warwickshire Regiment

Bill Bowdidge, he was a corporal, in this place where I got wounded and Bill, he was wounded at Lebisey and he was wounded on the same day as me. What happened was he got a bullet through the back of his shoulder, left shoulder, I'm lying next to him and this blood spurted up like a fountain from his shoulder. Topper [Private Steve Brown] was in this little barn, he comes out, he had a big wodge of antiseptic padding, puts it on his shoulder and knelt on it and the rest of us went into the lane and that's when I got wounded and Dave Honey got killed. It was very tough. But Topper knelt on this bloke for nearly three hours to staunch the blood and Bill said this bloke saved my life!

Dave Honey was killed by the same mortar that wounded me. [He] was on the left hand side of the lane, I was on the right hand side. The Germans were mortaring us, because they knew where we were, and they were very good at mortaring. As it got dark, three Churchill tanks came up...

Corporal Bill Bowdidge
9 Section Commander, 18 Platoon, D Company, 2nd Battalion, Royal Warwickshire Regiment

I yelled to my section, "spread out, get down." Immediately a bullet went through my left shoulder. I moved to the shelter of a farm wall where I was aware that a main artery was spouting like a fountain. I was quickly becoming very weak & I then realised nothing could save me, there were no stretcher-bearers, I knew for certain I would be dead in a few minutes. My first thought was for my mother & I thought she'll be devastated when she gets the news! Then a remarkable feeling of euphoria came over me, I would see bright lights & hear bird song. I was so happy & I thought what a wonderful thing it is to die, no pain, completely oblivious of the obvious noise going on. Then I was aware of Steve talking to me and the pain came back. He rolled me over on to my back & using his own field dressing he tightly bound up my shoulder & managed to stop the fountain. It was now dark & the farm building was burning, he lifted me up and carried me across a field where we came across a Churchill tank, the tank commander gave me a shot of morphine & they laid me alongside the turret. I was aware of being lifted down to be placed on a stretcher-carrying jeep, one of the bearers was an old friend who told me that it was 4 a.m.

Private Ted Bedford
D Company, 2nd Battalion Royal Warwickshire Regiment

It was also in August that my friend Corporal Bowdidge was severely wounded. I was told he had been killed and he assumed that I was also dead. It was a wonderful surprise to bump into each other at the Warwicks' church parade in 1993. We were able to go together to the 50th Anniversary of D-Day in France and we remained in regular contact until his death...

Private Walter Charles Gray
D Company, 2nd Battalion Royal Warwickshire Regiment

We said 'faye night' to each other, which meant fair enough, this is the end, and I went back to the lane where the attack started.

The War Diary of 4th Battalion Coldstream Guards recorded on 13 August:

> No.2 Sqn supported the Warcs of 185 Bde. Owing to heavy shell and mortar fire the Warcs suffered heavy casualties and were unable to get on. No. 6 Troop [Lieutenant Meinertzhagen] and No. 8 Troop, R. C. Carr-Gomm, did valuable work in bringing in wounded on their tanks. Then two troops remained with the infantry all night.[5]

Despite wounds to both his arms, his work was not complete, 'Nifty' Pettitt jumped up to direct the tank commanders along the lane, to avoid his wounded and fallen comrades. Once clear, he managed to clamber aboard the Churchill tank and take refuge in the turret, all to the sound of enemy machine-gun fire rattling against the thick armour of the tank.

Private Walter Charles Gray
D Company, 2nd Battalion Royal Warwickshire Regiment

The bullet, well that just went round to my throat you see, the bullet hadn't come out and when it hit me I was lying like that and firing and a jet of blood shot up like a fountain, and it went right over my shoulder, and then it just stopped dead. But it was strange really, because I saw it going right up, you know. Anyway we packed up and went back, and when we got back there were about four or five other wounded men, just sitting by the edge of the lane in front of the farmhouse, because we'd obviously captured the farmhouse, and, so we just, I just sat down, and then one of the chaps that I knew, he just stopped quick, and I had a little dressing and he put it round my neck, but the leg hadn't happened when we first

5 TNA WO 171/1251, '4th Battalion, The Coldstream Guards, War Diary.' August 1944

> got back, but he had to go because they were clearing up and everything, and then this shell came over and it hit me in the leg, and a lot of other wounded men got wounded again.
>
> ... anyway, so just at that time, after that happened, one of our tanks come up the lane and the sergeant got off, 'cause all the tank commanders were sergeants, and he got off and he had a quick look around, and funnily enough a German tank had started coming down the top, but he saw our tank and he went off quick, yeah, and the sergeant came and.... he got one of their dressings and put that on and he gave me morphine. He said I can put you under our gun if anyone wants to get up there and take you back too when we go, but if it has to fire it will kill you.

By this time though, there were only 16 men still fit under Major Bell, with a large number of wounded men in their care, including Captain Clarke. As the situation became desperate, the Coldstream Guards' Churchills arrived in strength and drove the German airborne troops back, forcing them south of the stream beyond Creully. A Company, in its support position was also taking casualties, including its commanding officer, Captain M. L. B. Hall. With so many men now out of action, it was impossible for them to hold their position, and D Company was ordered to fall back to the north-west of Creully, their original position. Major Barratt, Captains Hall and Clarke and Lieutenant Martin-Webb, plus 48 ORs were wounded in this action, 10 men were killed with one man reported missing.

Private Walter Charles Gray
D Company, 2nd Battalion Royal Warwickshire Regiment

> ...I only spent six weeks fighting. I was taken to a field and the tanks formed a circle to protect the wounded.... once when I was lying down I saw Germans by a hedge. I told the sergeant and he fired a shell at them and killed them. I was lying in a shallow ditch and the ground came up and hit me in the nose and it was pouring with blood. We didn't have a change of clothes so I would have been looking pretty awful!

Private Dennis Pettitt
D Company, 2nd Battalion Royal Warwickshire Regiment

> Neither of us should have been there, before we went from England, Tom Bundock, the Major, called us into his office and said we should be going soon, and we should be in the front line. You, Pettitt, are technically too young, and you, Honey, are too old, he said, but the infantry needs as many as it can get, so you can volunteer if you wish, you needn't volunteer and nobody would think the worse of you. Of course, we both volunteered, and we both got wounded together, same day, same mortar, poor old Dave, I can see him now. His wife came from Ladywood, Birmingham, he died on the Sunday evening and his wife had sent a telegram that morning, to celebrate the birth of a son, that's how cruel war can be.

Corporal Bill Bowdidge
9 Section Commander, 18 Platoon, D Company, 2nd Battalion, Royal Warwickshire Regiment

> ...hardly a day passes without thinking of him [Steve Brown]. I could not have lasted long with a severed main artery and it was at least eight hours before I received medical attention. He saved my life. All my possessions were incinerated at the field hospital; Steve would have been in a bit of a mess too. I was flown home to a hospital in Swindon in hospital pyjamas, my only souvenir being my dog tags. My pay book followed by post.

Private Walter Charles Gray
D Company, 2nd Battalion Royal Warwickshire Regiment

> Well it made me a cripple, I mean when I came out the army I had to have a walking stick, I came out with crutches and a walking stick, and I have been disabled ever since. You know, my leg made me walk with a stick, so it was long lasting.... what they did when I got in the hospital, they took some skin off here (indicates right leg) and covered the hole up, but you could still see the bones through the skin, they were all cracked and that, anyway, I got transferred to another hospital... called Barts and they were in St Albans. They were the ones who were making new faces for people, so they were plastic surgeons...

Following this engagement, another round of reorganisation was required and on 14 August, 99 greatly needed reinforcements, including Lieutenant R. J. Keast and 2nd Lieutenant C. H. Mavin, arrived the day before to populate the ranks of A Company, but even with these new arrivals, the battalion was forced to reduce further to just two rifle companies. The troops remaining from the other companies were brought together as a newly formed D Company under Captain Bell, with the platoon commanders being Lieutenant Moxham, Lieutenant Roberts, and the Canadian, Lieutenant Keast. A Company remained under the command of Major Brock, with Lieutenant Jarvis, Lieutenant Tennant and 2nd Lieutenant Strutt as his platoon commanders.

On the 15th, after the bruising encounter they had gone through, the 2nd Warwicks found the front line now swiftly moving away from them, as the combination of US Forces advancing rapidly from the south against limited resistance and British and Canadian divisions holding out against German counterthrusts and repelling the attackers, put the enemy into retreat at a far greater pace. This afforded the men two days of relative peace to take stock and rest, before moving to a concentration area south-east of Tinchebray on the 17th in the luxury of countryside unspoilt by battle. Here, the battalion settled in for a period of recuperation and importantly, more training.

A series of promotions were made on 17 August. Captain Bell became acting major, Lieutenants Allen, Jarvis & Moxham becoming acting captains, with Acting Captain Allen permanently appointed to the role of adjutant in the absence of Peter Batt. Amongst the training there were two causes for celebration on the 19th: Lieutenant F. A. E.

Bonney was awarded his MC and an MM was awarded to Corporal A. Church, for their gallantry on Gold Beach on 6 June while serving with the 2nd Battalion Hertfordshire Regiment. Also, the battalion football team defeated the 2nd KSLI team 3–1.

Revd. Austin held a Sunday church service for all ranks on the morning of 20 August. That afternoon, the final of the 185th Brigade football tournament was held, with the battalion taking a 7–1 victory over the team fielded by Brigade HQ.

Divisional training now took on a new focus, with special reference to river crossings, convincing the men their next task would be to cross the Seine in an advance north of Paris. Troops of Churchill tanks from the Scots Guards also joined the men for their training on 22nd, in a concerted effort to improve close infantry armour cooperation. It was during this period that the infamous Falaise Gap was closed on the remaining troops of German Army Group B encircled in the pocket. Approx. 50,000 German troops were captured, with more than 10,000 being killed in the period 12–21 August.

Major T. L. Brock
Officer Commanding A Company, 2nd Battalion Royal Warwickshire Regiment

> Some very useful training was carried out in conjunction with a squadron of Churchills from the Scots Guards. We were given the task of preparing for the crossing of a major river obstacle, which was thought to be the Seine, and a lot of planning was done. However, the general advance was so rapid that we were never called upon to carry out this task.

The week before, on 18 August, Lieutenant Colonel Jerram, CO 1/7th Battalion Royal Warwickshire Regiment, received the news that the 59th Infantry Division, was to be disbanded, along with the brigades and battalions within. 1/7th had fought bravely since landing in Normandy, and had taken considerable casualties of their own – 551 between 8 July and 16 August alone. Understandably, the unhappy news was not well received, but the available manpower in the UK to draw reinforcements from was limited, the barrel had been scraped. As such, it was necessary for one division to be broken up and 59th Division held least seniority, and thus it was sacrificed. The men of the infantry battalions would be dispersed as replacements into the other divisions. With the 2nd Battalion down to only two rifle companies, Lieutenant Colonel D. L. A. Gibbs saw this as his battalion's opportunity to secure reinforcements from the regiment. Word was received on 23 August that two companies, 16 officers and 299 ORs of the 1/7th would arrive on the 25th to bring the 2nd Battalion up to full strength. While Lieutenant Colonel Jerram returned to England as commander of Divisional Battle School, Captain D. F. Horsfall, 2nd Lieutenant R. K. Harris and 18 ORs joined HQ Company 2nd Battalion. Lieutenant F. Nankivell and 11 ORs joined the men of A Company. Major F. C. Butterworth, Captain W. J. Phillips, Lieutenants F. Clayton, D. E. Hosker, D. E. Plater and 107 ORs now formed B Company. C Company was reformed with Captain A. C. Gilbert, Captain P. V. Dorman, Lieutenant F. G. MacRae, Lieutenant D. B. Brown, Lieutenant E. P. Withers and 110 other ranks. Captain Bell's D Company received Lieutenant R. G.

Bennett and 16 ORs to bolster its ranks. And finally, Captain J. R. Allen, Lieutenant M. Wood and 27 ORs joined the Support Company.[6]

The now combined battalion of the Royal Warwickshire Regiment immediately returned to training, there were however many absences as groups of the men were afforded the opportunity for 3 days' entertainment at the corps and divisional rest camps. As the month came to an end, orders arrived with instructions for the battalion to move north of the Seine early in September.

25 August 1944, D+80, was momentous for another reason. In the early hours of this Friday morning, American troops of the 4th US Infantry Division commanded by Major General Raymond Barton entered the streets of Paris in the wake of uprisings within the city that had started on 19 August. *Generalleutnant* Dietrich von Choltitz, Military Governor of Paris and commander of the German garrison surrendered to representatives of the Free French provisional government, this was swiftly followed by a victory speech from *Général* de Gaulle. During planning, Monty had committed his forces to strict phase lines on the map, identifying the geographic advances that should be achieved within specific time periods. According to these phase lines, Paris would be liberated on or by D+90. So, while some may still bemoan the Allies failure to take Caen and Bayeux on D-Day itself, the ultimate success of the invasion is clear with Paris being liberated a full 10 days in advance of the plan.

With the Nazi grip in France weakening, rumours swirled on the subject of fighting the Japanese and the BLA (British Liberation Army) became known as 'Burma Looms Ahead' to many, as men of the battalion wondered if they would be joining their sister battalion in the Far East.

A mix of training, reinforcement and recuperation continued, with regular cinema shows and the men rotating away from the ranks to spend time at divisional club and rest camps established by 1st Corps and 2nd Army. 3 September saw the fifth anniversary of Chamberlain's declaration of war, a parade service was held to remember the sacrifices of those years. That evening, at 1800 hours, motor transport arrived to take the battalion to their next destination, some 240km away at a concentration area near Gisors, in a series of villages to the north-west of Paris and on the north bank of the Seine, with the entire battalion arriving by 0800 hours the following day. From there, billets were arranged in any available space, usually barns. Battalion HQ, A Company, S Company and HQ Company were dispatched to nearby Villers-en-Vexin. The village of Vatimesnil was the destination for B, C & D Companies. Once again, the detail involved in the move order is fascinating, and now out of the immediate front line, military discipline reigns supreme once more, insisting that: 'All troops will be properly dressed at all times.'

Some of the more talented men had formed a dance band of some quality to entertain the battalion. On 9 September the Mayor of Villers-en-Vexin hosted an officers' dance which the band performed at, much to the enjoyment of all who attended. The following day, A Company's barn home was converted into a dance hall, for an all-ranks dance,

6 TNA WO 171/1387, '2nd Battalion, the Royal Warwickshire Regiment, War Diary,' 25 August 1944

to which the citizens of Villers-en-Vexin were invited, possibly the younger female residents of the village were a motivation for holding the dance too. These enjoyments did not hinder the training and smooth running of the battalion, training programmes covering carrier transport, mortar and signals use, as well as patrolling and river crossing were all covered in detail.

Major T. L. Brock
Officer Commanding A Company, 2nd Battalion Royal Warwickshire Regiment

> This proved to be by far the most pleasant area in which we had so far been. Here it was possible to house the whole battalion under cover for the first time since D-Day. We were also able to organise excellent recreation in the form of dances, football and visits to Paris, in addition to the usual visits to the divisional club and cinema. The dance band was reformed and proved most popular.
>
> The battalion will probably long remember its stay at Villers-en-Vexin and the hospitality it received from the villagers, in particular *Monsieur Le Maire*, M. Cheron.
>
> A considerable amount of training up to company level was carried out and it was not long before the battalion began to pull itself up to its pre-D-Day state of efficiency and ready to take part in fresh battles. It was here that Capt. H. C. Illing MC, having recovered from his wounds, returned, and was appointed adjutant.
>
> This really was an excellent state of affairs when one considers that the battalion had suffered very heavy casualties during the Normandy battles.

Captain Harry Illing MC re-joined the battalion on 11 September, taking over responsibilities as adjutant from Captain A. R. Allen. Small parties were able to visit Paris on 11 and 12 September, however future trips were cancelled as orders arrived informing Lieutenant Colonel Gibbs that the battalion should be prepared to move at short notice. However, no immediate departure was evident and after a rehearsal parade on the 13th, General Sir Lashmer Gordon Whistler, GCB, KBE, DSO & two bars, the divisional commander, inspected the battalion on 14 September. The inspection was followed by an ENSA show that evening, which was greatly appreciated by all who attended.

On the 18 September 1944, after travelling almost 250km in the last four days, the 2nd Battalion Royal Warwickshire Regiment finally left France, crossing the Belgian border to the north of Mons, passing the battlefields of the last war. The War Diary poignantly states:

> 'THIS WAS THE FIRST ENTRY INTO BELGIUM SINCE 1940.'

10

Conclusion

This story, the actions and fate of these men, is not uncommon throughout all regiments and battalions within the Allied forces landing in Normandy and fighting their way inland. However, the overriding aim of my work was to highlight the largely neglected involvement of this historic regiment in the narrative of the Second World War, while also serving to dispel common misunderstandings and myths that abound. Firstly, that the focus on Caen was flawed and that subsequently Operation Goodwood was a complete failure. Secondly, to provide clarity of which troops actually relieved the airborne troops at what are now the Pegasus and Horsa Bridges.

There is no question that it took far longer than anticipated to take Caen and that losses during Operation Goodwood were great and that the objectives that Monty had suggested were not all achieved, but the overarching success of this approach was that the German forces were purposefully drawn onto the Caen sector away from the US Forces further south, allowing the latter the space to manoeuvre and the ease of passage to make their great advances forward, and that the Royal Warwickshire Regiment were a key facet of this operation's success.

General Omar Bradley
Commanding Officer, US First Army

> While Collins was hoisting his VII Corps flag over Cherbourg, Montgomery was spending his reputation in a bitter siege against the old university town of Caen. But had we attempted to exonerate Montgomery by explaining how successfully he had hoodwinked the German by diverting him towards Caen from the Cotentin, we would have given our strategy away.
>
> We desperately wanted the Germans to believe this attack on Caen was the main Allied effort. But he nevertheless left himself open to criticism by overemphasising the importance of his thrust towards Caen. When Monty failed to take it, the correspondents blamed him for the delay.[1]

1 Alexander McKee, *Caen: Anvil of Victory* (London: Souvenir Press, 1964)

Perpetuated by the film *The Longest Day* our overriding image is of Lord Lovat relieving Richard Todd's Major Howard on the Orne/Caen Canal bridges. As we have already discussed, brave and excellent soldiers though they were, Lovat's commandos of 1st Special Service Brigade were not the first beach landing troops to reach Major Howard, that honour went to small elements of the Royal Engineers and of 2nd Battalion The East Yorkshire Regiment, and neither did they actively relieve the beleaguered men on the bridges. Absolutely they arrived, but continued on their own vitally important mission, and it was D Company of the 2nd Battalion Royal Warwickshire Regiment that, on being diverted from their original objective, relieved 7th Parachute Battalion on the bridges, holding a greatly extended defensive line overnight before intervening in the horrific battle at Lebisey Wood the following day. We can and should be proud of the knowledge it was D Company of the 2nd Warwicks who deserve the honour of this place in history.

Private Dennis Pettitt
D Company 2nd Battalion Royal Warwickshire Regiment

> We got to Benouville, Pegasus Bridge, in the early afternoon of D-Day. People say to me, 'You couldn't have been on the beach and at Pegasus Bridge,' 'Oh couldn't we? Read the war record and you'll see that we were.' They say, 'No, it was the commandos.' I say, 'Look, I wasn't in the commandos, and I can tell you, we, the 2nd Battalion, or at least D Company, were.' I remember having a little skirmish, an argument with a bloke on the bridge. He said, 'Are you a veteran?' I said, 'Well yeah.' 'What were you in?' I said, 'The Royal Warwicks.' He said, 'What are you doing here then?' I said, 'Because we were here on D-Day.' 'You weren't,' he said! They just couldn't believe you could be on the beach and then three or four hours later you could actually be where the paras had dropped, they just couldn't see it. There's not many people who can claim they did both.

In a wider focus, there is a preponderance in more recent times to downplay the achievements of D-Day and the Normandy campaign, to belittle the contribution and ability of the defenders of the Atlantic Wall in some abhorrent agenda to suggest the Allied feat of arms was somehow inevitable, that as long as they turned up, they would be victorious. There is also that post war attitude of denigrating British military events and figures in favour of appeasing former allies and adversaries. This is not to say we should not be ashamed of the dark points in the history of empire, and nor does it cast aspersions on other belligerents of the Second World War. Whatever their ideology, German soldiers (and men in German uniform) fought bravely and showed equally astonishing levels of heroism in their own right. Italian Troops engaged Allied forces in North Africa ferociously, especially considering they had been so poorly supported by the Fascist government of *El Duce*. French forces were not defeated because of a lack of skill and bravery of their soldiers, but by the abysmal tactics and policies of their governments between the wars and in the face of Blitzkrieg. The Russians waged a war incomparable in sacrifice and brutality to that of the Western European theatre of operations. Canadian, Australian, New Zealand, Indian and all Commonwealth soldiers, sailors and airmen fought with gallant ferocity in theatres far from their own home, many of them never to return. US Forces introduced a new approach of military might, achieving feats unimaginable to many at the time, even as Canadian and British forces bore the brunt of the German defensive ability around Caen. However, the British public should be able to remain proud of the achievement of our armed forces, especially during the Second World War, the vast majority of whom were civilians in uniform, not pre-war professional soldiers. Those men and women achieved things both near and in far flung corners of the world that are unimaginable to most of us today. This is not about celebrating the defeat of another nation, but of remembering the sacrifices made by so many. So many of whom have been forgotten in their own family's history.

As the initial focus of this short work, Corporal Charlie Tweed, my hero, perished in Normandy, I will end the narrative here. This by no means spelled the end of the war for the men of the Royal Warwickshire Regiment. In the two months following the Normandy landings, the 2nd Battalion Royal Warwickshire Regiment officially recorded losses of 218 young men killed and 368 wounded, and the slog continued for another eight long months.[2] They would soon move on to The Netherlands in the wake of Operation Market Garden, where bitter fighting would continue, with particular ferocity around Venraij. After a freezing winter on the Maas, further battle honours were won for The Rhineland, Lingen, Brinkum and Bremen once the battalion had crossed the Rhine and finally entered Germany before VE Day could finally be celebrated. One day, I, or hopefully a more capable author, will pick up the narrative where I have halted, to continue the story of the men of the Royal Warwickshire Regiment who lived, fought and died in conditions and circumstances modern generations cannot comprehend. It is to those men, indeed all Allied personal, to which we should be thankful, to remember and honour their sacrifices.

When you go home
Tell them of us and say
For your tomorrow
We gave our today

2 There are 196 names listed in the Roll of Honour included within this work, many of the men who were officially listed within the 218 killed above were not on active service with the battalion at this time, and were serving in other capacities with Commando battalions or other such entities.

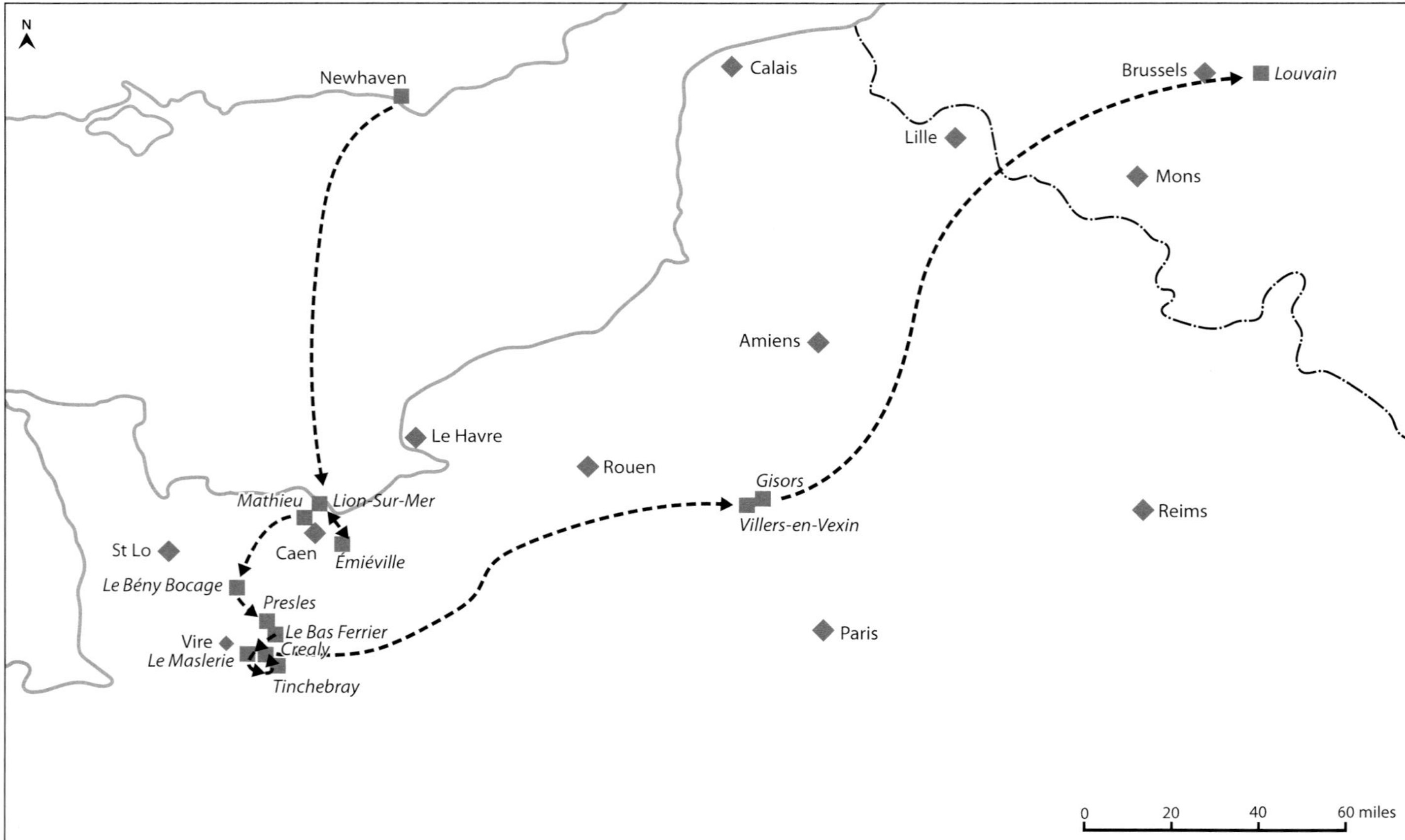

The approximate route travelled by 2nd Battalion Royal Warwickshire Regiment between 5 June and 18 September 1944.

11

After the War

Captain Peter Aubrey Batt

After being wounded in Normandy in August 1944, Peter was flown back to England, where he spent the remainder of his service on officer selection, before being discharged in 1947. Returning to his hometown of Rugby, he returned to accountancy and was offered a partnership with the local firm of Howkins and Harrison, where he stayed for the rest of his working life. He was a Rugby Councillor for two decades, Mayor of Rugby in 1959–1960 and became a Freeman of the Borough in 1974.

Peter was passionate about young people having opportunities and served as President of the Rugby and District Scout Council for 40 years, as well as being a former Warwickshire County Director of the St John Ambulance Brigade. He also joined the Rotary Club of Rugby in 1961 and was President in 1977–1978. He took a keen interest in the activities of the Rugby Branch of the Royal Warwickshire Regimental Association. At a regimental dinner in Warwick to commemorate the 50th anniversary of D-Day, he was thrilled to be reunited with one of the two men who had carried him to safety in France all those years before.

Peter and his wife Jean had three sons: Philip, James and Stephen, and six grandchildren. Aged 82, Peter died on 17 February 2003.

Private Sir Dennis Pettitt

After being wounded twice in Normandy Dennis was transferred to service in the Sudan with 8th Battalion Royal Warwickshire Regiment, from where he returned home to Birmingham after the war to take up a trade as an electrician. There he met his wife Dorothy, and also introduced his friend Steve 'Topper' Brown, who had been 2nd Battalion's sniper, to his family. Topper went on to marry Dennis' sister Bette.

Dorothy had been born in Nairobi, Kenya, and an opportunity arose to move there after the war in the 1950s. Dennis became involved in the independence movement, and served as Vice President of the Kenyan League.

Daughters Lynda and Jocelyn were born in Nairobi, but the family returned to the UK as Lynda had been diagnosed with spina bifida. Back in the UK, sons Nicholas and Robert were born in the 1960s.

Dennis served on Birmingham City Council, campaigning for improvements to services for disabled people. His trade was by now a lift engineer for Express Lifts, and he was promoted in 1968 to regional manager in Nottingham, where the family moved.

Dennis continued his local government service and was elected to Broxtowe Borough Council and then Nottinghamshire County Council in the 1970s. He was to go on to become the Leader of Nottinghamshire County Council for 20 years.

He also served as UK representative on the EU Committee of the Regions, and often spoke about how his wartime experience had left him determined to work for a peaceful and compassionate Europe. After the fall of the Iron Curtain, he worked with a fledgling democratic local government in Poland, and was awarded the Polish Commander's Cross by Lech Walesa, and given the freedom of the City of Poznan.

He was knighted in 1998 at Buckingham Palace, by Her Majesty The Queen, for services to Local Government and the Community.

He retired from local government in 2001 and was able to commit more time to volunteering with the Royal British Legion, becoming President of the Eastwood & District Branch, and an active member of the Nottinghamshire Normandy Veterans' Association. He returned to Normandy many times over the years to remember fallen comrades. Sir Dennis Pettitt passed away on 16 January 2011, aged 85.

Private John Gundy

Following the Normandy campaign, John served in France, Belgium, Holland and Germany, being involved in the liberation of the death camps. Although he was injured by shrapnel at one point, he continued to serve, and his final role was in the peacekeeping mission in Palestine until 25 August 1946.

He married his wife Dorothy (nee Frampton) in 1944, and they had two children, Andrea and Phillip. After the war he lived in Alum Rock, Birmingham and worked as a welder until 1979, when he retired to Somerset. His grandchildren include Deborah, Sadie, Lindsay, Adam and Sam. The youngest, Sam, has also served in the forces, in the RAF.

In 2007, his eldest grandchild Deborah produced a short film about his time during Operation Overlord, funded by the Veterans Challenge Fund. Inspired by the scrapbook he had kept during the war, 'Finding Buck' traces his return to the battlefields of France – to visit places he saw, to remember the events he experienced and to find the resting place of a friend and comrade-in-arms, Albert 'Buck' Buckley. The film was originally distributed on DVD free to schools and libraries in Somerset and surrounding areas and can now be viewed on YouTube. The original scrapbook forms part of the exhibition at the D-Day Museum in Portsmouth and other items from his time in the army were also donated to the museum service.

He passed away a year after the film was made, in May 2008.

Private Walter Charles Gray

Walter, known as Wally by his family and friends, was read the last rites in the field hospital in Normandy and although he was left disabled and in need of a walking stick, he defied all odds and went on to live a long and full life.

Initially he worked in the Ballito Hosiery Mill in St Albans, before joining his Uncle Stan as a painter and decorator, a career he carried on independently well beyond retirement age.

In 1947 he was married to Jean Lesley Shipp, they went on to have three daughters, seven grandchildren and at the time of his passing he had 11 great-grandchildren, his family still continues to grow.

He was awarded the *Légion d'Honneur* in 2014 by the French government in honour of his services during the Normandy landings and his role in securing the liberation of France.

Although he never returned to Normandy, he would have liked too. He was very humble about his war service and always said he didn't do anything special.

Wally departed this life on 24 April 2022.

Lieutenant-Colonel Denis Lucius Alban Gibbs, DSO and Bar

Lieutenant Colonel Gibbs was awarded a bar to his DSO for strong leadership of the battalion during the battle for Venraij. After the war, he commanded 1st Battalion, The Queen's Royal Regiment from January 1947, in Singapore, until September 1948, in Berlin when the 1st & 2nd Battalions were amalgamated. He was Commandant of Eaton Hall Officers Cadet School until he retired from the Army on 18 October 1950, and died on 27 April 1984.

Brigadier Harry Illing CBE, MC and Bar

After re-joining the battalion, Major Illing served as adjutant in The Netherlands, and then again as a company commander in Germany. In April 1945 he led his company in an assault on Leeste, near Bremen and was awarded a bar to his MC. He married his fiancée, Janet MacDonald the same year. Illing served in Korea until 1954, whereupon he was posted to HQ Malaya command, before serving with distinction in Aden, Malaya, Hong Kong and then in Germany as part of the British Army of the Rhine. He was awarded the General Service Medal with campaign bars for Palestine 1946–1948, the Canal Zone, Malaya (where he was Mentioned in Dispatches) and the Arabian Peninsula (which was for service in the Aden Protectorate). He was Depot CO of the Royal Warwickshire Regiment in 1956 and appointed 1st Battalion CO in 1962, continuing that role when the regiment became the Royal Warwickshire Fusiliers in 1963.

As a brigadier, he was appointed to lead the British Military Mission to Aden/South Yemen, and in 1967 was commander of the Hong Kong and Kowloon garrison. He served as Commander Rhine Area of the British Army of the Rhine and his final military command was as OC 51st Infantry Brigade. He was appointed CBE and retired from the Army in 1975. Illing was Deputy Colonel of the Royal Regiment of Fusiliers for Warwickshire from 1974 to 1981.

He wrote a short but excellent account of his activity in Normandy on 6 & 7 June 1944 up to when he was wounded, re-joining the account as the battalion left France and entered Belgium and The Netherlands. His book, *No Better Soldier,* is available from the Fusiliers Museum in Warwick and is essential reading for anyone hoping to understanding the perspective of an infantry officer in Normandy 1944, and I have relied on his words greatly.

Harry passed away aged 90 on 10 May 2011.

Captain Alastair Bannerman

After a long journey by cattle truck, on 22 August 1944 Alastair arrived at *Oflag 79*, near Braunschweig. He kept himself occupied entertaining his fellow inmates, directing plays and giving poetry readings.

Alastair kept a beautifully written diary, addressed to his wife Elisabeth, which has been referenced throughout this work. Upon capture, the diary was confiscated, Alastair never expected to see it again. In 1948, the diary was miraculously returned, via the regiment, by a member of the 21st Panzer Division that had captured him on 7 June and had kept hold of it. Incredibly, a second copy of the diary was returned in 1964, via the Inspector of the German Navy and the British Naval attaché in Bonn.

Pre-war, Alastair trained at the London Theatre Studios featuring in a number of theatre productions including John Gielgud's famous 1937 Queen's Theatre season, and playing Oberon to Renee Ascherson's Titania at Oxford Playhouse just before joining up in 1940, after having also appeared on television. After release from captivity he returned to the stage, being part of the original cast of Rattigan's *The Winslow Boy* for the entire West End run, touring with the Oxford Playhouse and the Phoenix Theatre. He featured in the film *Trapped by the Terror* in 1949. Then with a final burst at the Lyric Hammersmith with Flora Robson in the original production of Shaw's *Captain Brassbound's Conversion* in 1950 before returning to the family textile business in Manchester

After leaving the textile industry, Alastair found success with his open air plays and 'Fetes Champetres' at Stourhead, he became National Events Manager for the National Trust and retired to Beaminster in 1984, where he put on church shows, painted, wrote poetry and told and retold tales of his life on stage and at war.

He and Elisabeth returned to Normandy with a Royal Warwickshire Regiment party for the 50th anniversary of D-Day in 1994.

Captain Bannerman passed away on 6 February 2009, aged 94.

Alastair's wartime diary was published in 2014 and featured in the ITV documentary 'If I Don't Come Home – Letters from D-Day,' it is still available as an eBook.[1] HRH, William, Prince of Wales, read from the diary in his remembrance speech during the D-Day 80th anniversary celebrations in 2024.

Lieutenant Colonel Kingston St John Adams

After recovering from his wounds 'Tiny' Adams would remain with the Royal Warwickshire Regiment as a regular soldier after the war. He was promoted Captain in 1948 and was Mentioned in Dispatches in 1949 for his work as Battalion Intelligence Officer with 1st Battalion in Palestine.

He married his wife Monica in 1952, and they had two sons and two daughters together.

In 1954, while stationed in the Suez Canal Zone he was made Adjutant of the 1st Battalion and was promoted to Major in 1955. His final military role was as GSO1 in the British Military Mission to Saudi Arabia in 1973–1978, retiring in 1978 as a Lieutenant Colonel.

After the sad death of his wife, he remarried in later life to Angela. He passed away on 20 August 2013.

Corporal Bill Bowdidge

While still in hospital, Bill was discharged from the army in April 1945, a galling situation for a professional soldier. His treatment continued into 1947. Once recovered he worked in a builder's office as a clerk, eventually rising to become a quantity surveyor, while also spending 26 years in the Royal Observer Corps.

He was fanatical about motorcycles, and riding with a modified clutch to accommodate his damaged arm, attended many motorcycle events, including the Monaco Grand Prix; through which events he was introduced to Eileen, whom he married in 1952.

Bill was also a keen athlete; after the war, running with his damaged arm in a splint, he ran a number of half and full marathons including the 1988 London Marathon.

He was instrumental in organising the 1994 'Hampshire Remembers D-Day' event, where he was able to meet and reminisce with a number of former Warwickshire Regiment colleagues.

Bill saw an article in the newspaper in 1998 about his old friend 'Nifty Pettitt' receiving a Knighthood and was able to contact him via his constituency office. Bill wrote to Dennis with an incredible account of his time in Normandy which has been invaluable in this work.

1 Alastair Bannerman, *If I Don't Come Home, Letters from D-Day* (London: ITV Ventures, eBook, 2024).

Appendix I

2nd Battalion Royal Warwickshire Regiment, Roll of Honour Normandy Campaign 6 June – 18 September*

Name	Date	Age
Private Thomas David Aitkin	7 June	18
Private George Frederick Amos	7 August	26
Private John Herman Anderson	19 July	29
Private James Arch	2 August	25
Private Lionel Frank Arnold	13 August	18
Private Benjamin Aston	8 July	27
Private William Arthur Baker	7 June	Unknown
Private Robert Owen Barnard	12 August	20
Private Douglas Barber	5 August	25
Private James Halsell Barker	7 August	26
Private Walter Leonard Bastard	24 July	28
Private Cecil Edward Bavin	30 July	19
Sergeant George Herbert Beadle	7 June	29
Private Gordon Bennett	6 August	18
Private John Bennion	20 July	25
Private Bernard Bleasdale	7 August	30
Lance Corporal Arthur Henry Boswell	2 July	24
Private Bert Boulstridge	25 July	24
Private Percy Cyril Bowers	8 July	24
Lance Corporal Sydney Bowler	21 June	29
Private Robert Edward Brewer	25 June	27

Private David James Brown	6 June	22
Private George Brueton	23 June	23
Private Reginald Charles Bryant	13 August	19
Private John Thomas Bryant	20 July	35
Private Albert Buckley	7 June	19
Major Thomas Gordon Bundock DSO MC	6 August	25
Private Thomas Burdett	14 June	24
Private Alfred Charles Butcher	23 July	30
Private Cyril Byron	13 August	18
Private Brian Churchman	19 July	20
Private Hubert Victor Clack	24 July	19
Lieutenant Lawrence Cohen	8 July	22
Private Clifford Lloyd George St John Collins	20 July	32
Private Edward Cyril Compton	8 July	19
Private Gerrard Coogan	8 July	18
Private Victor George Copson	20 July	27
Private John Richard Cowley	20 July	30
Private George Crabb	9 August	33
Private John Crowther	25 July	31
Private Brindley Dally	12 August	29
Private Frederick L Davies	20 July	34
Lance Corporal Frederick Alfred Deeming	5 August	24
Private Frederick Dewitt	8 August	28
Lance Sergeant George Dipper	7 June	28
Lance Sergeant James Dix	7 June	29
Lieutenant Alan Dockerty	7 June	21
Private Lawrence Frank Drake	23 June	24
Private Arthur Dunn	19 July	19
Private Cyril Ede	19 July	31
Private John Frederick Ellis	6 August	31
Private Donald Arthur Elston	7 June	18
Private Edward Ensor	24 July	23
Private John Fields	15 August	23
Private Arthur Ford	8 July	28
Corporal Jack Albert Fowler	6 August	27
Lance Corporal Ronald V. Fowler	7 June	25
Private Francis William France	8 July	27
Private Douglas Stuart Friend	25 July	23
Private Donald Fryer	4 August	23

Private James Gardiner	2 July	32
Private Arthur Henry Garwood	7 July	26
Private Thomas Glen Ruthven Gillespie	18 July	23
Lance Corporal Robert Gillmour	6 June	32
Private Ralph Gomm	6 June	28
Corporal Walter George Goody	8 July	23
Private Joseph Gray	12 August	31
Private Percy Harold Greatrex	12 August	42
Corporal John Green	25 June	28
Private Norman Greensides	7 June	28
Private Thomas Henry Griffin	6 August	32
Private Harry Robert New Griffin	7 June	26
Sergeant Kenneth Grimsey	6 August	34
Private Frederick Haines	7 June	19
Private William Hall	7 June	26
Private Donald Harbone	27 July	19
Corporal Kenneth Albert Harding	8 July	29
Private Derek Harley	8 July	19
Private Alfred Donald Harris	19 July	30
Private Herbert Richard Harris	5 August	19
Private Thomas John Harvey	20 July	18
Corporal Levi Heames	7 August	24
Lance Corporal Frederick Heeler	24 July	28
Lieutenant Colonel Hugh Owen Seymour Herdon	7 June	38
Private Kenneth John Hinton	20 July	23
Private Terence Hippisley-Cox	6 August	18
Private Earnest Hodcroft	9 June	27
Private David Honey	13 August	36
Corporal David Henry Hopkins	7 June	30
Private Leslie Horne	8 July	19
Private Frederick William Horton	6 June	24
Private George Joseph Howard	8 July	18
Private Cyril Alfred Hudson	18/19 July	31
Private Charles Edward Hughes	4 August	32
Private Harold Joel Hughes	7 August	26
Private Robert Frederick Hughes	7 August	31
Private George Edward Hulatt	12th August	35
Private Jack Hulley	19 August	21
Private Raymond William Humphries	7 June	18

Private Bernard Hunsley	8 July	24
Private Walter Jaffrey	21 July	28
Private William James	8 July	28
Private Kenneth Charles Henry Jennings	7 August	18
Private John Idwal Jones	6 August	26
Private Ronald Victor Jones	6 June	28
Sergeant Francis Eric Jones	6 June	27
Corporal Ronald William Jones	7 August	24
Private Joseph Jones	7 June	22
Private Raymond Jones	7 June	20
Private Douglas Joseph Jones	8 July	26
Lance Sergeant Robert Keeley	7 July	28
Private Herbert Isaac Kimmins	8 July	19
Sergeant James Thomas King	8 July	25
Private William Cyril Kingston	14 August	36
Private William Joseph Lambert	14 August	24
Private Norman Lane	6 June	20
Lance Corporal Gerrard Patrick Lee	9 July	26
Warrant Officer 1 William Lewis	4 August	36
Private William Henry Lingard	6/7 June	27
Private John Madden	9 July	24
Corporal Reginald David Marks	13 June	34
Private Albert Marshall	17 July	19
Private Herbert Martin	8 June	25
Private Kenneth Mason	8 July	19
Private Frank McDowell	8 July	20
Private Robert Merrick	7 June	19
Corporal William Millard	20 July	23
Private Arthur Miller	19 July	27
Private Stanley Mills	8 July	28
Corporal Albert Mullineux	20 July	37
Corporal Davis Mullis	5 August	25
Private Wilfred Douglas Nash	25 July	30
Private Leslie William Newcombe	8 July	32
Corporal Harold Newey	4 August	24
Private John Gilbert Daniel Newnham	12 August	26
Corporal Ronald Owen Nicholls	7 June	33
Private Thomas Henry Pain	7 June	24
Private Joseph Parker	7 June	28

Private Alfred Leslie Parsons	7 June	19
Private Lewis George Patience	14 June	24
Corporal Edward James Pay	14 June	26
Private Arthur Pearson	20 July	30
Private Cyril Perkins	20 July	24
Private Robert James Phipps	7 August	21
Private Ronald George Presswell	19 July	22
Private Leslie Price	7 August	26
Private Harry Prigg	8 July	25
Private James Gerrard Quigley	8 July	19
Private John Randall	20 July	24
Private David Albert Rawlings	6 August	29
Private Ronald Arthur Rimes	7 June	24
Private Alan Roberts	19 July	17[1]
Private Emlyn Roberts	7 June	28
Private John Roberts	8 July	30
Private Earnest James Robinson	20 July	19
Sergeant Leonard John Rouse	6/7 June	37
Private Walter Richard Rumsey	9 July	21
Private Alfred John Russell	8 July	23
Private Clifford Sagar	7 August	22
Private Joseph Sale	24 July	18
Private Ronald Sheppard	26 July	23
Private George Shipley	5 August	35
Private Wesley Walter Short	4 August	32
Private Charles Leonard Taylor	24 July	19
Private Albert Henry Thomas	14 June	32
Private Howard Thomas	26 August	19
Private Archie Thompson	12 August	22
Private Bertram James Timmins	2 July	24
Private John Tinsley	6 August	28
Private Kenneth Roy James Treadwell	8 August	19
Private William George Trotman	26 July	21
Private Mathew Tullett	7 August	24
Corporal Charles Tweed	19 July	23
Lance Corporal Anthony Lawrence Vinicombe	25 July	20
Private Thomas Wagstaff	13 August	24

1 Recorded on his CWGC headstone as 19 years old.

Lieutenant Victor Walton	7 June	30
Private Raymond Ware	6 August	19
Private Thomas Welch	20 July	26
Private Henry Richard Welham	25 July	30
Private Desmond Howard Wells	20 July	37
Private George Wells	6 August	30
Private Kenneth Alfred Wesley	21 July	29
Private Joseph Baden Wheeler	20 July	19
Sergeant William Henry Whitehall	8 July	26
Private Lawrence Whittaker	13 August	21
Private John Wilkes	7 June	26
Private Stanley Williams	6 August	31
Lance Corporal Thomas George Wilson	22 July	27
Lieutenant Arthur George Wilson	7 June	28
Private William Wood	15 August	34
Private Ebenezer Frank Wood	19 July	26
Corporal Ralph Wright	14 August	22
Private Sidney Yates	6 August	33
Private Thomas Anthony Yeomans	20 July	18
Private Dennis James Young	12 June	22

*Details from Commonwealth War Graves Commission Files

Appendix II

3rd British Infantry Division – Order of Battle

GOC: Major General T. G. Rennie

8th Infantry Brigade:	1st Battalion The Suffolk Regiment 2nd Battalion The East Yorkshire Regiment 1st Battalion The South Lancashire Regiment
9th Infantry Brigade:	2nd Battalion The Lincolnshire Regiment 1st Battalion The King's Own Scottish Borderers 2nd Battalion The Royal Ulster Rifles
185th Infantry Brigade:	2nd Battalion The Royal Warwickshire Regiment 1st Battalion The Royal Norfolk Regiment 2nd Battalion The King's Shropshire Light Infantry

Machine Gun & Heavy Mortar Battalion: 2nd Battalion, The Middlesex Regiment

27th Independent: Armoured Brigade	13th/18th Royal Hussars (Queen Mary's Own) 1st East Riding Yeomanry The Staffordshire Yeomanry
Royal Armoured Corps:	22nd Dragoons 3rd Reconnaissance Regiment (8th Battalion Royal Northumberland Fusiliers)
Royal Artillery:	7th Field Regiment RA (9th, 16th & 17th/43rd Field Batteries) 33rd Field Regiment RA (101st, 109th & 113th/114th Field Batteries) 76th Field Regiment RA

	(302nd, 303rd & 354th Field Batteries) 20th Anti-Tank Regiment RA (41st, 45th, 67th & 101st AT Batteries) 73rd & 93rd Light Anti-Aircraft Regiment (218th & 322nd AA Batteries)
Royal Engineers:	17th, 246th and 253rd Field Companies RE
RAMC:	8th, 9th and 223rd Field Ambulances RAMC
Royal Signals:	3rd Division Signals
Provost Company:	3rd Division Provost Company
1st Special Service Brigade:	No. 3 Commando No. 4 Commando No. 6 Commando No. 45 (Royal Marine) Commando
4th Special Service Brigade:	No. 41 (Royal Marine) Commando

Appendix III

Landing Timetable, 6 June 1944

Beaching Time	Unit	Marching Troops	Vehicle Parties	No	Vehicle Type	Craft Serial	Craft Type
H+60	2nd Royal Warwicks	6				228	LCI(L)
H+150	2nd Royal Warwicks	176		33	Bicycle Airborne	314	LCI(L) Mk II
H+150	HQ 185th Brigade	2				314	LCI(L) Mk II
H+150	'L' Section Div Signals	2		1	Handcart WT	314	LCI(L) Mk II
H+150	7th Field Regt SP	4				314	LCI(L) Mk II
H+150	3rd Recce Regt	3				314	LCI(L) Mk II
H+150	17th Field Coy RE	6				314	LCI(L) Mk II
H+150	223rd Field Amb	6				314	LCI(L) Mk II
H+150	'A' Bombardment Troop	3				314	LCI(L) Mk II
H+150	2nd Royal Warwicks	178		47	Bicycle Airborne	315	LCI(L)
H+150	223rd Field Amb	7				315	LCI(L)
H+150	17th Field Coy RE	6				315	LCI(L)
H+150	253rd Field Coy RE	9		7	Bicycle Airborne	315	LCI(L)
H+150	2nd Royal Warwicks	185		33	Bicycle Airborne	316	LCI(L)
H+150	223ed Field Amb	6				316	LCI(L)

Beaching Time	Unit	Marching Troops	Vehicle Parties	No	Vehicle Type	Craft Serial	Craft Type
H+150	253rd Field Coy RE	9		9	Bicycle Airborne	316	LCI(L)
H+240	2nd Royal Warwicks		31	2	Carrier Universal	338	LCT(4)
H+240	2nd Royal Warwicks			2	Gun 6pdr AT	338	LCT(4)
H+240	2nd Royal Warwicks			2	Carrier Mortar	338	LCT(4)
H+240	2nd Royal Warwicks			2	Carrier Universal	338	LCT(4)
H+240	41st Anti-Tank Bty	6	14	2	M10 (3" AT)	338	LCT(4)
H+240	41st Anti-Tank Bty			1	Carrier Universal	338	LCT(4)
H+240	253rd Field Coy RE	2	3	1	Angledozer D7 (armd)	338	LCT(4)
H+240	15th Field Pk Coy RE			1	Trailer 18 ton Carrimore	338	LCT(4)
H+240	'L' Section Div Signals	5	8	1	car hy utility Humber 4x4	338	LCT(4)
H+240	'L' Section Div Signals			2	Car 5 cwt 4x4	338	LCT(4)
H+240	'L' Section Div Signals			2	Handcart	338	LCT(4)
H+240	HQ 185th Brigade	3	3	1	Car 5 cwt 4x4	338	LCT(4)
H+240	2nd Royal Warwicks		37	2	Carrier Universal	339	LCT(4)
H+240	2nd Royal Warwicks			2	Gun 6pdr AT	339	LCT(4)
H+240	2nd Royal Warwicks			3	Carrier Mortar	339	LCT(4)
H+240	2nd Royal Warwicks			2	Carrier Universal	339	LCT(4)
H+240	2nd Royal Warwicks			1	Car 5 cwt 4x4	339	LCT(4)
H+240	41st Anti-Tank Bty		14	2	M10 (3" A tk)	339	LCT(4)
H+240	41st Anti-Tank Bty			1	Carrier Universal	339	LCT(4)
H+240	'A' bombardment Troop		2	1	M3A1 White 15 cwt 4x4	339	LCT(4)
H+240	2nd Middlesex		25	5	Carrier Universal	339	LCT(4)

Beaching Time	**Unit**	**Marching Troops**	**Vehicle Parties**	**No**	**Vehicle Type**	**Craft Serial**	**Craft Type**
H+240	241st HQ Provost Coy		1	1	Car 5 cwt 4x4	339	LCT(4)
H+240	2nd Royal Warwicks	7	26	2	Carrier Universal	340	LCT(4)
H+240	2nd Royal Warwicks			2	Gun 6pdr AT	340	LCT(4)
H+240	2nd Royal Warwicks			2	Carrier Mortar	340	LCT(4)
H+240	2nd Royal Warwicks			1	Carrier Universal	340	LCT(4)
H+240	'L' Sec Div Sigs		3	1	M14 (US halftrack)	340	LCT(4)
H+240	3rd Recce Regt		2	1	Car 5 cwt 4x4	340	LCT(4)
H+240	2nd Middlesex	1	34	1	Carrier Universal	340	LCT(4)
H+240	2nd Middlesex			6	Carrier Lloyd	340	LCT(4)
H+240	2nd Middlesex			6	Trailer Mortar	340	LCT(4)
H+240	2nd Middlesex			1	MC	340	LCT(4)
H+240	17th RN Beach Sig Sec	5		1	Handcart	340	LCT(4)

Bibliography

Archives

Imperial War Museum

IWM 32512, Allan, John (Oral history), 6 March 2009
IWM 18512, King, Russell (Oral history), 21 September 1998
IWM 18577, Meredith, Berkeley Donald (Oral history), 6 March 2009
IWM 10880, Pugh, Alec Graham (Oral history),13 September 1989

Royal Regiment of Fusiliers Museum, Warwick

Adams, Kingston St John, Letter dated 30 June 1944
Brock T. L., 'Account of the Battalion in Normandy, Holland & Germany'
Gibbs, D. L. A., Letter dated 11 July 1944
Gibbs, D. L. A., Letter dated 16 July 1944
Gibbs, D. L. A., Letter dated 30 July 1944
Illing, Harry, Letter dated 18 June 1944
Kreyer, Robin, Letter dated 21 June 1944
Kreyer, Robin, Letter dated 3 August 1944

The National Archives

WO171/182, '185th British Infantry Brigade, War Diary,' June–September 1944
WO171/1251, '4th Battalion, The Coldstream Guards, War Diary,' August 1944
WO219/3075, '3 British Infantry Division Group Landing Timetable,' 19 March 1944

Pettit Family Archive

Bowdidge, Bill, Letter dated 5 January 1994
Pettitt, Dennis, Video Interview, 2009

Smalley Family Archive

Tweed, Charles, Letter dated 19 June 1944

Stephens Lee Family Archive

Lee, Adrian, 'Death of my 2nd Warwick Father'

Private Collections

Adams, Kingston St John, 'Personal account of the Normandy Landings'

Illing, Harry & Adams, Kingston St John, 'Presentation notes, Historical Association Rugby Branch'
Illing, Harry, 'Battlefield Tour Guide Notes'

Published Books

Bailey, Roderick, *Forgotten Voices of D-Day* (London: Ebery Press, 2009)
Baldwin, Frank, *D-Day Gunners* (Barnsley: Pen & Sword Military, 2022)
Bannerman, Alastair, *If I Don't Come Home, Letters From D-Day* (London: ITV Ventures, eBook, 2024)
Blandford, Edmund, *Two Sides of The Beach* (Shrewsbury: Airlife Publishing Limited, 1999)
Carell, Paul (pen name of Paul Karl Schmidt), *Sie kommen!: Die Invasion 1944* (Oldenbourg: Gerhard Stalling Verlag, 1960)
Cunliffe, Marcus, *History of The Royal Warwickshire Regiment 1919–1955* (London: William Clowes and Sons, 1956)
Dalglish, Ian, *Battleground Europe Operation Bluecoat* (Barnsley: Pen & Sword Books, 2003)
Delaforce, Patrick, *Marching to The Sound of Gunfire* (Stroud: Alan Sutton Publishing Limited, 1996)
Delaforce, Patrick, *Monty's Iron Sides* (Stroud: Sutton Publishing Limited, 1995)
Dunphie, Christopher, *The Pendulum of Battle Operation Goodwood 1944* (Barnsley: Pen & Sword Books, 2004)
Field, Jacob, *D-Day in Numbers*, (London: Michael O'Mara Books Limited, 2014)
Fisher, Stephen, *Sword Beach* (London: Bantam, 2024)
Ford, Ken, *Battle Zone Normandy: Sword Beach* (Stroud: Sutton Publishing Limited, 2004)
Ford, Ken, *D-Day 1944 (3): Sword Beach and The Airborne Landings* (Oxford: Osprey Publishing Limited, 2002)
Ford, Ken, *Caen 1944* (Oxford: Osprey Publishing Limited, 2004)
Hastings, Max, *Overlord* (London: Michael Joseph Limited, 1984)
Hoeller, Hans, (Andreas Hartinger, ed.), *D-Day Tank Hunter*, ([Germany], Privately Published, 2022)
Illing, H. C., *No Better Soldier* (Warwick: Privately Published, ND)
Isby, David, *The German Army at D-Day* (London, Greenhill Books, 2004)
Jones, Geraint, *D-Day The Unheard Tapes* (London: MacMillan, 2024)
Keegan, John, *Six Armies in Normandy* (London: Jonathan Cape Limited, 1982)
Lincoln, John, *Thank God and The Infantry* (Stroud: Sutton Publishing Limited, 1994)
Mayo, Jonathan, *D-Day Minute by Minute* (London: Short Books, 2014)
McKee, Alexander, *Caen: Anvil of Victory* (London: Souvenir Press, 1964)
Pearce-Smith, Kenneth, *Adventures of an Ancient Warrior* (Lymington: Privately Published, 1984)

Rommelaere, Guy (Shirley Wallis, trans.), *The Forgotten Massacre* (Warwick: Warwick Printing, 2001. Original French edition, Privately Published, 2000)
Sadler, John, *D-Day The British Landing Beaches* (Stroud: Amberley Publishing, 2019)
Scarfe, Norman, *Assault Division* (London: Collins, 1947)
Shergold, David, *Critical Hours on D-Day* (Sutton Coldfield: Boldmere Press Limited, 2024)
Trew, Simon & Badsey, Stephen, *Battle Zone Normandy – Battle for Caen* (Stroud: Sutton Publishing Limited, 2004)
Trigg, Jonathan, *D-Day Through German Eyes* (Stroud: Amberley Publishing, 2020)
Von Luck, Hans, *Panzer Commander* (New York: Praeger Publishers, 1989)
Williams, Andrew, *D-Day to Berlin* (London: Hodder & Stoughton, 2004)
Zetterling, Niklas, *Normandy 1944* (Winnipeg: J.J. Fedorowicz Publishing, 2010)

Published Journals and Newspapers

Atherstone News, 4 August 1944
The Antelope, The Journal of The Royal Warwickshire Regiment. (2004 Edition)
The Antelope, The Journal of The Royal Warwickshire Regiment. (2005 Edition)
Coventry Telegraph, 11 July 1944
The Nuneaton Chronicle & Midland Farmers Gazette, 2 November 1923

Electronic Resources

Batt, Peter, 'Old Rugbian Day 1995, VE Day 50th Anniversary (1995)'
http://www.youtube.com/watch?v=Lue4xR4OOu0, accessed 14 January 2023
Richardson, Deborah, 'Finding Buck'
http://www.youtube.com/watch?v=AbPGEBbWIoE, accessed 8 October 2023